FLUTTER POINT

FLUTTER POINT

ESSAYS

ERIK ANDERSON

ZONE 3 PRESS

Clarksville, Tennessee

ZONE 3 PRESS | Clarksville, Tennessee

Copyright ©2017 by Erik Anderson

FIRST PRINTING

Library of Congress Cataloging-in-Publication Data

Names: Anderson, Erik, 1979- author.
Title: Flutter point : essays / Erik Anderson.
Description: Clarksville, Tennessee : Zone 3 Press, 2017.
Identifiers: LCCN 2016032552 | ISBN 9780990633327 (softcover : acid-free
   paper)
Classification: LCC PS3601.N54332 A6 2017 | DDC 814/.6--dc23
LC record available at https://lccn.loc.gov/2016032552

ISBN: 978-0-9906333-2-7

Book and Cover Design by **David Bieloh**
Cover Art: "The Sight" ©2012
by **Jeremy Moss** (www.jeremymoss.org)

A Tennessee Board of Regents Institution

Better that we are ugly, but we are here.

Haitian proverb (trans. Edwidge Danticat)

Nonself, I suppose, is an apt description of the human condition.

Eula Biss

CONTENTS

IN THE ANTHROPOCENE

Our early ancestors climbed out of the oceans only to climb, much later, into the trees. That they eventually climbed down again has made all the difference and, conversely, no difference at all. This is what concerns me.

*

In 1916, a man named Madison Grant published a tract of scientific racism that became one of Hitler's favorites. *The Passing of the Great Race* never took hold in the United States, but Grant wielded influence in another arena: he helped to found the Bronx Zoo, among other things, and from 1925 to 1937 was the director of its overseeing body, the New York Zoological Society. This is hardly a coincidence, writes Alexandra Minna Stern: "the apparition of eugenics," she says, "sits restlessly at the heart of American environmentalism."

*

Civilization is an interglacial phenomenon, made possible by the retreat of the ice sheets some 12,000 years ago. All of human culture—all literature, all religion, all wars—takes place as though between two parentheses. While much encourages us to see our lives, and our species, as central—as the culmination of various processes that led, individually and collectively, to us—the truth is that our interval on the planet may be a digression. An afterthought, a curiosity, an addendum to the body of the text.

*

For a figure like Grant, saving white America from the threats of an open society was little different from saving the redwoods from the lumber companies. He saw the biological world as in need of salvation and so divided it into threats and the threatened. Grant's racism may have been quickly discredited, but the *othering* at the heart of his gesture was not. The spectacle of the zoo is one of its extensions. Environmentalism, in some of its forms, is another.

*

Geology is an impractical science. The numbers it deals in are larger than our imaginations, and its most profound implications, like those of astrophysics, derive from our inability to situate their chronology. Because such time is beyond our capacity to conceive it, the scale of our understanding will always be modest. Its objects are just too unworkable. Imagine a watch that kept time by the epoch. Each hand would be stuck on the Anthropocene for your entire life, and your children's lives, and their children's lives, and so on. Of course, much of the clock face would be blank, but that's another problem entirely.

*

From Grant's time to our own, we've held tightly to the idea that the planet can be improved by human ingenuity, but the mechanics of nature—our tremendous store of knowledge notwithstanding—are demonstrably beyond our control. Two days before "the largest climate rally in history" was held in Washington, DC, a meteor struck Siberia. It was the same day an asteroid named DA14 was predicted to stage a dramatic flyby. Though it was widely and dissonantly reported that the two events were unrelated, many outlets nonetheless reminded us that a similar collision did in the dinosaurs.

*

Besides, the evidence runs counter to the wisdom: everywhere we have gone we have brought destruction with us. From the beginning, we have tipped every ecosystem we have entered out of balance. We don't even know how many species have gone extinct as a result of our rise to dominance. The number is likely so large as to be meaningless. That is to say, larger than we can bear.

*

At dinner with the science writer, it is agreed that we are animals, albeit ones adept at building things, relationships among them. Intelligence may be a product of complex social structures, but there's hubris in making too much of our sophistication. 99.9% percent of species that have ever lived have gone extinct, and there's no reason to think we are immune. Someone at the table suggests that with artificial intelligence life is evolving beyond itself, but the science writer doesn't buy that. Life, she says, is more marvelous than any machine.

*

Others argue that humans may become a mechanism for seeding life in outer space. It's as delightful an idea as it is unlikely. But even if we become capable of propelling ourselves to habitable planets—and we are nowhere close to this—we will not have solved the problem of us. We will have merely deferred it.

*

It had been my intention to attend the climate rally, and I can give no good reason why I didn't. Instead, I wrote a check, put a sticker on my car, shared certain petitions online. I couldn't be bothered to drive the two hours to DC on a frigid Sunday when the house was warm and there was beer in the fridge.

*

Maybe it's better to say that one can situate oneself between two glaciers or between one day and the next, but not both—or only with great difficulty. Put another way, the living of any specific life may be incommensurable with what we know about living in general. The rules of the quantum world do not apply to the interstellar one, and vice versa, and though scientists have worked feverishly in recent decades to reconcile the two, one suspects that it will all end up a black hole.

*

Literature, music, art—surely these differentiate us from the animals? The bowerbird is an artist, the science writer says. Whales delight in their songs.

*

As for the rally, I might have been unwilling to trade in short-term convenience for long-term relief. But it's equally true that the organizers— most environmental groups, for that matter—have yet to get the message right. I'm not exactly sure what that right message is, but given the audacity of thinking we can save the planet, I would argue it has less to do with protecting polar bears and honeybees—noble as these intentions are—than with protecting ourselves. I have yet to hear enough arguments that appeal to my *animal* self-interest. I worry, for our collective sake, that by the time I do it will already be too late.

*

If the 4.5 billion year history of the planet were reduced to a single day, all of human history would fit into the last few seconds before midnight. Indeed, we might be, in more ways than one, the ball dropped on the Earth. But geologic time also defies linearity. The cycles are large and unpredictable, and though we know it's now contracting, when the ice will swell again is anybody's guess. The only thing we know for certain is that someday, if history is any indication, it will.

*

It is only on the genetic level that humans are not an interglacial phenomenon: our DNA has marched uncannily along from the primordial soup in which the first cell divided. It's a wonderful legacy, and a humbling one. Our lives are so much larger, biologically, than us. "All life is one," Bill Bryson writes. "That is, and I suspect will ever prove to be, the most profound true statement there is."

*

The closing parenthesis may take any number of shapes—a meteor, an eruption, a pandemic—but that it will take shape seems likely. We may outsmart it for a time, but eventually it will bracket us off, elegantly, economically—under a mile-thick layer of ice, perhaps. In light of our prospects, maybe you have to do the same with the death of the species that you do with your own: either accept it or convince yourself it isn't there. But the latter may be a bit like a clock that never comes full circle. And nature abhors nothing as it does a straight line.

*

The animal question is not the only one that matters, but it is the one from which, at this point in our history, all others derive. No attempt to address the anthropogenic effects of our presence will come to anything unless we first disarm the *othering* that governs our world.

*

If I am an animal, what does that mean for the animals? What does my animality mean to me?

*

If I am an animal.

To whom does the lamp communicate itself? The mountain? The fox?
Walter Benjamin

A few days into spring, and already summer, my wife and I started watching *Project Nim*, James Marsh's documentary about a chimpanzee raised as a human. That we were doing so during a March heat wave—what one science writer called "an unprecedented event since modern US weather records began"—was as distressing as the fact that, a few minutes into the movie, my wife was enraged: not only had the infant chimp been removed from its mother, but it had been necessary to sedate her in order to pry the baby from her hands. Halfway through, my wife was so irritated by almost everyone in the film we had to turn it off. I admitted there was little about the story that wasn't shameful, but I still went to bed sulking about the interruption. In the morning she apologized: she had taken it all rather personally, she said. For whatever reason, it had been impossible for her to suspend her judgment, and though it wouldn't be true to say she felt Nim's story as her own, she felt its helplessness, and its cruelty.

In 1973, Nim was taken from the primate research center in Oklahoma where he was born to New York City, where a graduate student named Stephanie LaFarge raised him among her own children. The research project, conducted by a Columbia psychologist, Herbert Terrace, was designed to answer the question of whether chimpanzees, with whom humans share 99% of our DNA, could acquire language. More specifically, could a chimp form a sentence? Nim was tutored in American Sign Language, first in his adoptive human household, then in a lab at Columbia. But the study had baggage: namely, a long-standing debate between those who theorized language as a set of rules hard-wired into the human brain, and those who argued it was a tool developed toward specific ends. It's telling that, in terms of this debate, Terrace's mentor at Harvard was B.F. Skinner, the noted behaviorist, and that Nim's given name—Nim Chimpsky—was a dig at Skinner's chief critic, and the theorist of universal grammar, Noam Chomsky.

The results were ambiguous. Nim learned a substantial number of signs, 125, but Terrace concluded that his use of language was an elaborate form of begging. Watching the film, one immediately questions the findings, however, in no small part because Terrace comes off as arrogant and indifferent. Another caveat comes in a milder form of my wife's initial reaction: the situation is patently absurd, and this is nowhere more evident than in the scenes in which one tutor, Laura-Ann Petitto, struggles to potty train a diapered Nim. This is part of Marsh's considerable craft as a filmmaker: he draws our attention to what's disturbing without ever naming it explicitly. I have trouble imagining a viewer, for instance, who would not see the events of 9/11 hovering behind Marsh's earlier film, *Man on Wire*, which recounts the story of Philippe Petit, the French aerialist who conducted a high-wire walk between the twin towers as construction was drawing to a close. Marsh never mentions their destruction because each image of the towers implies their absence. Likewise, he does not exaggerate the senselessness of Nim's predicament because all it takes is an image of a chimp in diapers to establish it.

Terrace's study ended abruptly around the time Nim turned five. That it had failed to definitively answer the questions it set out to ask was less pressing a concern than the fact that Nim had already attacked several of his tutors, including one woman who had a portion of her face torn off. No doubt there were other reasons—fatigue and lack of funds among them—but the growing strength of a young male chimp was as convenient as any. From the grounds of the mansion owned by Columbia, where he was then living, Nim was returned to the Oklahoma center where he was born. The scenes are dramatic: chimpanzees in cages, shouting loudly, and Dr. Bob Lemmon, the center's director, carrying a cattle prod at his side. It was at this point that my wife's patience eroded completely. We turned off the TV, shut the windows—although it was still, at 9 p.m., rather warm—and went to bed.

When we started up again the following night, it was clear we had been too hasty. The years Nim spent in Oklahoma appeared to have been good ones, relatively speaking. They were far better than the years that followed. When financial pressures prompted the center to sell some of its chimps, it found a willing buyer in the Laboratory for Experimental Medicine and Surgery in Primates (LEMSIP), a facility affiliated with NYU's School of Medicine. Along with hundreds of other chimps housed at LEMSIP, Nim became the subject of vaccine experiments. In 1995, NYU closed the facility, and many of the chimps were simply moved to comparable laboratories; others were rescued by LEMSIP's chief veterinarian, Jim Mahoney, who placed over a hundred in sanctuaries around the country. By then, Nim's case had received some public attention, and, having been purchased by the Fund for Animals, he was moved to a sanctuary in eastern Texas.

Near the end of his relatively short life, Nim's surrogate mother from the beginning of the film, Stephanie LaFarge, comes to visit. He remembers her, but how could he have forgotten? She breastfed him, after all. LaFarge enters Nim's enclosure, against the advice of everyone present, and Nim lets loose on her, grabbing her by the ankle and swinging her from side to side. He nearly kills her and, in so doing, himself. Just as his warders are deciding whether or not to shoot him, Nim walks away. The reenactment is painful to watch, but it oddly reflects the opening of the film, in which Nim is removed from his biological mother. The forced separation from the latter is not the abandonment by the former, but that Nim's is in part a maternal tragedy speaks to my wife's frustration. Broken bonds, and imposed ones, are the unfortunate frames of Nim's life.

It's tempting to read *Nim* as a warning. Animals ought to be left in the wild, or it's better to learn from them in their own environments, à la Jane Goodall. These are entirely sensible, if conventional, conclusions to draw. But watching the film I thought, almost immediately, of Werner Herzog's *Grizzly Man* and its controversial subject, Timothy Treadwell, who for more than a decade spent his summers living among Alaskan grizzly bears. Much of Herzog's film consists of Treadwell's own footage, and as disturbing as it is to watch him sob or rage on camera, it's more disturbing that he treats the bears as though they were human. He talks to them, gives them names, and interprets their interactions through a distinctly human lens. There's a fetishistic quality to his approach: at one point he kneels down to feel the warm stool left by one bear on a rock. His delight is funny but troubling, and when, at the end of his final summer, Treadwell and his girlfriend are eaten by a hungry bear, it's clear that breaking some taboos can still have dramatic consequences.

This strikes close to the heart of *Project Nim*. Treadwell's experience teaches us less about grizzlies than it does about Treadwell and the ways each of us, to varying degrees, views the world through an anthropocentric, if not anthropomorphic, lens. Treadwell's commitment to protecting the bears only softens the biblical dynamic in which humans are given dominion over nature; it does nothing, despite Treadwell's good intentions, to revise that dynamic. In his twenty-six years, Nim likewise became a subject of (or to) human experience. His life, like the lives of Treadwell's grizzlies, was a screen onto which humanness was projected, and so what began as an effort to bridge, or address, the gap between human and animal did not end in a closing of that distance but a confirmation of it. In this way, too, Nim's story reflects Treadwell's: in both cases the distance appears to collapse only to expand once more, with violence.

The problem, as Giorgio Agamben argues, is not the inevitable separation between one species and another, but rather the shifting articulations of that separation, which not only establish our difference but give it its power and its presumptuous centrality. What exactly life would look like in a suspension of humanness isn't obvious, but one question the prospect raises is whether we can conceive of prerogatives that are not specific to given classes, so that no distinction prevails between human and animal rights. Does a chimp have as much claim to life and liberty as a human? And, if so, what obligations do we have to the chimps?

Little encourages us, day to day, to see nonhuman phenomena—the nature of chimpanzee societies, for instance—as possessing equal value to our own habits and preoccupations. The prolonged study and appreciation of the nonhuman world has become professionalized and largely consigned to the academy; apart from alarming articles about the consequences of climate change, science reporting is essentially marginalized. Even the *New York Times* ghettoizes the field: its dedicated section appears on Tuesdays, part of a rotating series that puts science on a par with style. This isn't precisely news. That our species is self-centered, that we see ourselves as occupying a divinely ordained position, is all too evident in the legions of animals we enslave for food and, paradoxically, in the naïve naturalisms that place the grand vistas of national parks on romanticized pedestals. Both are made possible by the division that defines our place in the world. Big-horn sheep don't marvel at the mountains. No cow cultivates other animals for food.

But it's hardly inevitable that this division should lead to, say, experimentation on chimps. Nor was the extraordinary heat of that March an unavoidable side effect of human habitation. Instead, the winter heat wave felt like Nim in another form: Nim writ large on the planet. In neither instance have we been able to reconcile our intelligence with the creaturely world. We have imposed or sought signs of our intelligence in that world, or we have assumed that this intelligence is resourceful enough (or divine enough) to sustain us. Hubris has always been central to tragedy, and that we persist in experimenting on chimps—as of this writing there are over a thousand in American laboratories—or fueling our lives with extracted carbon, may be a product of our species-specific variety: ever since Eden we have named and, in naming, divided.

For Walter Benjamin, this is a great comfort. Nature's muteness, he writes, is mournful, and even in the rustling of leaves, he senses a lament, the sadness of which lies in the inability to name. There have been few minds as nimble as Benjamin's, but he was working at a time before we knew that dolphins (among others) chatter with one another toward specific ends. He writes:

> Man communicates himself to God through name, which he gives to nature and (in proper names) to his own kind, and to nature he gives names according to the communication that he receives from her, for the whole of nature, too, is imbued with a nameless, unspoken language, the residue of the creative word of God…

An encouraging proposition, maybe, but it runs counter to the evidence. Nim named and his life was a sad one. Among other chimps, Nim would have been far from mute, even if his communication with other chimps had lacked names. I'm inclined to reverse Benjamin's formulation and to say that the name is a lament, in which case human sadness may reside in the inability to access what Benjamin calls the unspoken language of nature, the muteness that persists not within species but between them.

My wife was rightfully bothered by the treatment of the chimps in *Project Nim*, but it was the way this treatment reflected on humans that I found most disturbing. What does it say about us that we are not only willing to impose our language on another species, but that we see as inevitable the imposition of human names on the totality of the planet? Terrace's experiment does not prove the superiority of human intelligence any more than it disproves Noam Chomsky. All it proves is our loneliness. The story represents, on a small scale, a distinctly human shortcoming: we feel parentless, orphaned into our big, sophisticated brains. Unlike Benjamin, I don't see this isolation as mystical but self-imposed, and it only heightens the fundamental disjunction between us and the creaturely world. Again and again, we either try to articulate those differences or to eliminate them, but we must learn to mind the gap, not eliminate it. Situate ourselves inside the either/or, at the slash that, in its muteness, divides as much as it connects.

How does one inhabit a gap? And what does life look like there? If Nim's life is any indication, this in-between state—(n)either animal (n)or human—has its challenges and dangers. As immigrants know all too well, identifying with two (or more) incommensurable cultures can be a recipe for dissociation and violence, and although Nim exhibited both throughout his life, it's telling that his favorite activity was play—as though the gap he uniquely inhabited was, at best, a game. Of course, play can turn bloody, and the gap can be an invitation to violence, but there may be no better image for the position between the either/or—indicated by a diagonal line on the page—than that of the aerialist at work.

For his part, Petit says life must be lived at its edge, as though it were a high wire. One must practice danger and disobedience, foregoing safety and conformity. The wire is a state of contradiction: a path between two points that is never precisely used as such, and though it certainly is a route, the wire is its own destination. Death surrounds it, giving the walk its tension and beauty. Allow yourself fear and you've already fallen; instead, you must be entirely present, vigilant in your attention to the here and now. Human life presents its own bundle of contradictions, prominent among them the fact that, for a human subject, wilderness exists primarily in the abstract, as does, conversely, the wisdom suggested by our taxonomic name, *homo sapiens*. That our life consists of the movement between these poles, rather than a permanent residence in either, provides the ongoing tension and beauty of our existence.

If Nim's life means anything, in retrospect, it may be an exhortation to abandon the pole we superciliously cling to, and to accept that the opposite pole, to which our route that is not a route is also fixed, subjects us to certain entirely reasonable laws: those that govern, for example, the carrying capacity of a species (even, or especially, one with no natural predators). Given the warmth of the March during which we watched *Project Nim*—the warmth that promised only to increase—it is both imperative and unlikely we will do so.

Boom barrier. Boom, Belgium. Boom boat. Boom box. Boom brace. Boom burg.

Economic Boom. Boom end. Boomer Esiason. Boomerang. Boom fence. Boom Festival. Boom Gorge.

Boomier. Boomiest. Boomingly.

Boom-iron. Boom jigger. Kaboom.

Lars Boom. Latin American Boom. Boomlet. Log boom. Boom-man.

Boom mat. Boom method. Boom net.

Boom operator. Boom price. Boomslang. Boom-spar. Boom timber.

Sheer boom. Sonic boom. Boom, Texas. Boom value.

Boomy.

The subject isn't the boom exactly, but—to paraphrase Georges Perec—what there is around or about or inside it.

*

Captain Stalk comes over the intercom to introduce himself, First Officer Nilsson, and Bert, the flight attendant, who subsequently gives her safety spiel, including a prohibition I've never heard before: please refrain from chewing tobacco. She then announces that October is breast cancer awareness month and that the airline is running a fundraiser: buy a two-dollar glass of pink lemonade and the proceeds will be donated to research.

Nearly every passenger is a man, and they are mostly large and rough in one way or another. The three behind me are clean-shaven and well-dressed but also tall and solidly built. They spend much of the flight drinking and talking about guns. The portly man to my immediate right has a face covered in red stubble. He wears a Michigan Tech hoodie, and is built in such a way that he could have played lineman for their football team.

Cam, my fellow Michigander, tells me he's been working for three years in Williston, mostly for firms that service the equipment the oil companies use. He's from a place called the Keweenaw Peninsula, south of Houghton, which is, with the exception of Alaska, about as far north as you can get in the United States. He owns a hundred-acre farm there, currently managed by the oldest (at sixteen) of his seven kids. He had been a contractor at home, he tells me, but lost nearly everything in the recession. Now he's earning six-figures, hoping to be debt-free in five years, to retire in ten, but the work is taking a toll: four weeks in Williston, then four weeks at home, back and forth all year long. When he technically clocks in again at midnight, he can expect to be on the job at least eighty hours a week, sometimes as many as a hundred and twenty. He's worked shifts that have lasted twenty-six hours straight, and though the money's good, you miss out on important things in your life, he says, like sleep.

In articles about the oil boom, there's a stock character I might call the virtuous striver. His or her story enacts a familiar rags-to-riches arc in which one nobly struggles against all manner of adversity to save a house, provide for a family, achieve a better life. I see immediately that Cam is one of these, arriving in North Dakota in 2011 with the last of his cash, towing his camper with his truck, living in a farmer's field until the city annexed the land and the cops kicked him out. I don't envy his predicament, but there is something bogus in his narrative—the narrative that journalists have been peddling as well—at once a variation on and critique of the familiar American Dream. Even as "Cam" and the writers who chronicle him acknowledge the degree to which he has been left behind, they simultaneously celebrate his adversity. It is as though they were saying out of one side of their mouths, *look how terrible the economy is,* while out of the other, *look how wonderful.*

For his part, as he steps out of the plane, just before disappearing down the gangplank, Cam turns to me to say, *Welcome to the heartbeat of America.*

*

Driving around Williston that afternoon in my green Chevy Cruz, having been warned by the rental agency about damage to the windshield from the heavy truck traffic, I have the feeling that North Dakota is experiencing some version of the Brazil nut effect: all the people whose problems elsewhere are too large to handle wind up here.

In the Walmart parking lot, the license plates come from dozens of states, and groups of men in work gear and ball-caps, looking a bit like refugees, pile into or out of pickups. Later, north of town, I drive the wide dirt lanes of the Fox Run RV Camp. Perched on top of a hill, the place consists of long rows of improvised housing built from old campers and plywood and drywall. It reminds me of the slums I've seen in Mexico and Central America, places on the economic and societal margins where housing, like living, is improvised. And though in the preceding weeks I've tried to approach the boom with an open mind, I see a business sign shortly after leaving Fox Run that feels like the town's brand, in all senses: *Damage, Incorporated,* it reads.

That night I eat in a new restaurant attached to a hotel called El Rancho. Except for the shotguns mounted as door handles, the place is mallified enough that it could be anywhere in America. It is a brewery that doesn't brew beer with a mechanical bull you can't ride. The owners are trying to combine suburban life with the frontier—only it doesn't quite work. The music streaming through the speakers is what you would expect in an Old Navy.

After dinner, the sky is dark and I'm eager to head out into the oil fields, where I've heard it's possible to see gas flares dotting the landscape. I drive past a store with a giant neon sign that reads *Home of Economy*, but as soon as I'm out of town, it's as though I were driving through some controlled disaster. On the plane, Cam told me that coming into Williston at night is like landing on a birthday cake, the candles set out in every direction, but when I repeat the analogy to a local woman the following day, she tells me it's more like entering Armageddon. The flares are not only visible from space, their expanse is larger than Chicago's. North Dakota is on fire. And all of America with it.

*

Over breakfast, I scan the headlines in the *Williston Herald*. The big story is the death of a twenty-eight-year-old welder, a Marine veteran from Alabama who died earlier in the week. The article reports that North Dakota's worker fatality rate is higher than in any other state. It also includes the peculiar requirements for reporting incidents to the Occupational Safety and Health Administration: they are only to be disclosed in the case of a fatality or a "catastrophe," which is defined as the hospitalization of three or more people.

There are also two articles about a former local pastor, Jay Reinke, who opened his church's door to the city's large transient population, the demographics of which are elided in an accompanying article about the city's recent efforts to address the problem. The writers largely discredit Reinke, reveling a little in the collapse of his ministry, and highlighting both his admission to his wife that he had acted on homosexual impulses and his current job with Tractor Supply Company, visible, at a stretch, through my hotel window. One article ends by quoting the pastor at the Lutheran church, Mark Nicolaus, who stepped in after Reinke's resignation. The church has come back together, he says, and then, as though summing up the larger local dilemma, "We don't see anyone we don't know walking our halls."

In the half-hour or so I sit reading the paper, Fox News presiding over the proceedings, eleven people filter in and out of the breakfast area, all of them men of varying ages, all but two of them white. I read the obituaries, note the current count of active local oil rigs, 192, puzzle over the levels of and discharges from the nearby dam at Lake Sakakawea. It is October 11, 2014, and the weather caption on the front page predicts, strangely, "a little dose of spring," 64 degrees and sunny.

*

Roughneck (OED):

1. A person with rough manners; an uncultivated or uneducated person; (also) a quarrelsome troublemaker, a rowdy. Also *fig*.
2. a. Originally: an ironworker; (in later use also) a person engaged in any hard, rough, or poorly paid work; a labourer.
   b. A worker on an oil rig, *esp*. a labourer on the floor of a rig.

*

My room is a "suite," by which they don't mean a set of rooms but rather several rooms combined into one, and all of them, right down to the wall hangings (I hesitate to call them paintings), decorated out of a Pier One catalog. Upon entry, there's a full-sized fridge to the right, a hot plate built into the counter, a dishwasher and microwave, also built in. There's a tiled backsplash above the "kitchen" counter, which terminates in a slightly lower, L-shaped desk (and/or dining table) with a rolling office chair on one side and a matching dining chair on the other. Across from the desk sits a king bed ("the bedroom"), on one side of which is the bathroom wall and on the other an armless sleeper couch and accompanying faux leather ottoman. A TV sits atop a dresser on the opposite wall. The bathroom, a square within the rectangle, is notable only for the large walk-in shower, from which the bather is fully visible in the large mirror above the sink.

None of the patterns in the room match, nor the colors for that matter, though the green in the bedspread is picked up by the sleeper sofa, echoed in turn by the leaves on the curtains and valance, even in the bathroom walls, though you wouldn't know it, sitting in the main room. The appliances are black, with the exception of the white coffee maker, but the sink is stainless steel. The frames and light fixtures are a mixture of plastic brass and fake bamboo, including the full-length mirror across from the sleeper sofa but between the TV (still atop its dresser) and the L-shaped desk. The primary view through the window is of a new strip mall, still under construction. A dumpster sits in front of what will soon be a deli, the only business opening up in the building so far. It is beyond boring, architecturally, in the style of no style that dominates American suburban life, and for a moment it is difficult to tell the difference between the thriving place the developers have imagined and the abandoned one it someday may become.

And if one were to look inside my room from, say, the roof of the strip mall? Soiled clothes, draped across the extra chair, the sofa sleeper, and the ottoman: two pairs black dress socks, two pairs boxer-briefs, one pair of jeans (black), two t-shirts (one maroon, one blue), one sweater (maroon with white horizontal stripes), one dress shirt (blue and white gingham), one jacket (black). On the other surfaces, end tables, counter tops, etc.: one backpack (yellow and black), one tin of mints, gloves, stocking cap, ball cap ("Electro & Magneto, Service Since 1946"), a pencil sharpener, two coffee cups (ceramic), one 20-ounce bottle of water (mostly empty), one 22-ounce bottle of New Belgium IPA (empty), one glass with dried beer residue, two small notebooks (black), blue pen, Georges Perec's *Species of Spaces*, Francisco Goldman's *Interior Circuit*, a copy of the *Bakken Oil Business Journal*, a copy of the 2014 visitor's guide to Williston, the *Williston Herald* (Friday, October 10, 2014 edition), keycard, car key, wallet, phone, laptop, chargers. Beyond that are the objects that will remain after I have left: two telephones, a phonebook, alarm clock, guest services directory, remote controls, various pamphlets and placards listing the television stations or else reminding me not to smoke. The bed hasn't been made up, and the comforter is slumping slightly onto the floor. In short, the room is in slight disarray. I will attend to my share of it in due time. The housekeeper, whose cart I can hear moving in the hallway, will take care of the rest.

What can be said about a room like this—and there are thousands of them here—except that it is designed for one or more persons to live essentially as one would in a house, albeit in a room of roughly two hundred square feet, a room meant (unlike most hotel rooms) to imitate all the functions of home, a room so anonymous, so clearly in poor or missing taste, as to be any room, every room, and no room all at once. It is the ideal room in which to experience the ideal America being extracted from or projected on Williston, in which one might feel at home everywhere but, again to paraphrase Perec, at ease nowhere.

*

I spend the day with Ben, a friend of a friend and a Williston native. He pulls up to the hotel in a large black pickup, Credence blaring through the speakers, and we head to a couple of rigs drilling north of town. The sites are ugly things set against the tough but lovely land. The sky is big and bright and the derricks rise into it like monuments, but monuments to what? The drill pads are construction sites mostly, full of heavy equipment, portable trailers, and piles of pipe. I watch the horse heads on the pumping units nod up and down, John Fogerty's familiar voice in the background. It's just as Cam said: *the heartbeat of America.*

Ben is a voluble guy who drinks several sodas and a couple cups of coffee (double cream, double sugar) during the hours I spend with him. For work, he rents and services the heavy diamond bits (I pick one up in his garage) the oil companies—or rather, their intermediaries—use to drill deep into the ground, sometimes as far as four miles and always, in North Dakota, first vertically then horizontally. He drives all over the state and into Montana and South Dakota, but most of his clients aren't far away, no more than an hour and a half.

Driving back into town, he talks at length about the politics and practicalities of governing a city built for fifteen thousand but housing, he guesses, fifty-five. We pass a large red billboard that advertises "The Future of FR." "Fire-Retardant Clothing," he explains, translating the local patois—the oil companies require their workers to wear it. Ben expatiates on tolerance ("so long as they aren't trying to penetrate my ass, I don't care what they do"), on Texans ("they come up here with their big belt buckles, thinking they're better than everyone"), on the current American president ("this numb nuts"), on the prospects of a Republican one ("we need someone who isn't as old as the hill"), on the rumors of rapes in the aisles of the local Walmart ("I know what my town ain't"), and on the oil boom itself ("At this point it done more bad than good"). He's a warm, big-hearted guy, and even his bluster is delivered in the lilt of the upper Midwest, familiar to audiences of *Fargo*, and in a manner you might call North Dakota nice.

We have lunch in a place popular with locals called Dakota Farms. It looks like a Pizza Hut from the outside, but inside it's lined with log beams. The effect is strange, as though I were in both a chain restaurant and a local greasy spoon. Ben orders "the Chuck Wagon," a combination of eggs over easy, sausage, biscuits, and gravy that he mixes up into a hash. I order a grilled cheese with fries, and when I ask for some vegetables in my sandwich, both the waitress and Ben give me a funny look. Still, it's a pleasant lunch and Ben, in his generous way, insists on paying.

Afterwards, to establish some contrast, he takes me through the Williston of his youth: his middle school, high school, his church, houses where he went to parties. He points out the notorious side-by-side strip clubs, Whispers and Heartbreakers, outside of which a man was beaten to death in August. This part of town, he says, remains the same as he's always known it, with the exception of the heavy truck traffic that makes it nearly impossible to turn at some intersections. We head northwest of town, past Ben's early apartments. He was working construction back then, playing in a band on the side. There used to be nothing out here, he says, as we drive through miles of new apartment blocks and tract housing, all of it built in a sprawling, haphazard way, without any apparent plan, and in a style reminiscent of an ugly Denver suburb. *There used to be nothing out here.* He keeps repeating the line, as though reassuring us both that it's true.

*

On the Rhetoric of the Bakken Oil Business Journal (*Mary Edwards, Publisher*)

Fox News host, and two-time college dropout, Sean Hannity is "One Great American."

The "culprits" of the "real injuries inflicted on most tribal members" are "the Department of the Interior, the Bureau of Indian Affairs, the Bureau of Land Management, and the Environmental Protection Agency."

Of the last on that list: they're "on the wrong side of science."

Poverty can be "overcome" through "thorough resource management."

Indeed, "Fracking is as American as Apple Pie."

And "if fracking contaminates drinking water, it would have done so long before now."

"Meanwhile, one of the more harmful initiatives is Washington's war against coal."

The shale oil boom is an environmentalist's dream, having "by itself reduced global emissions more than all the well-intentioned solar and wind in the world."

Regarding local effects: "You won't hear many North Dakotans complaining," "North Dakota schools seem to work well under stress," and "the majority of North Dakotans embrace the industry's presence in the state."

On climate change: "We should think about embracing it."

On where the boom is headed: Montana.

On American intervention in the Middle East: "Drill, Baby, Drill!"

[sic, sic, sic.]

*

Later, I meet up with Lynn, a woman in her early sixties who owns a small engine shop downtown. She's more pessimistic than Ben—she's the one who calls it Armageddon—but then most people in her generation are, she says. Tell me why Target isn't coming to town? Tell me why we only have two grocery stores and they're both brimming? The big businesses aren't betting on Williston. They aren't counting on this lasting, and frankly she isn't either. There's a lot of anger, she tells me, anger at the pace at which the oil companies have been allowed to develop their leases, anger at the steep rise in property values and the high taxes that have resulted, anger at the transient workers who trash the town and the outside developers who have encouraged it all. Williston is bursting at the seams, and she has no intention of staying, though she's lived here her whole life. If her parents weren't still alive, she would have already left—for Phoenix, probably, which has often struck her as paradise.

One day, she says, there was a big fire overnight at a supply depot near downtown. It's not just that nobody told her there were toxic chemicals in the air and that she should stay in the house rather than drive to work, there was no way for her to know, no system to inform her. Meanwhile the city is racking up debt, running budget shortfalls that outstrip revenues by a hundred million dollars, and the profits are largely leaving the city, both in the pockets of the oil field workers and, more significantly, the companies that employ them.

Hanging on the wall behind her is a large, early-twentieth-century map of North Dakota. It's lovely to look at, I'm guessing eight feet by four, with a long water stain running from the upper right hand corner to the lower left. The map remains fairly accurate, she says, though it's also old enough that it omits several reservations. And if you get far enough out of town, as I do when I leave her shop, you can see why: much of the landscape of North Dakota is nearly as stark and empty as it was a hundred years ago— or, for that matter, two hundred years ago, when Lewis and Clark first reached the nearby confluence of the Missouri and Yellowstone Rivers. Maybe I just want to see that earlier North Dakota in the present one, to drown out the endless convoys of semi-trucks rolling down the highways and gravel roads, to wash away the tanks and derricks and pumps spoiling the horizon.

What is this nostalgia for the old map, this need to keep the land as it was? What *was* the land, if not shaped by human hands toward other ends? One of the stock phrases in the journalistic coverage, a line you hear repeated even by some locals, including Lynn, is that North Dakota has seen booms before. Usually people mean oil booms like the one in the seventies, but the pattern is older than that. Before there was oil exploration in the state, there was the Homesteading Act of 1862, which granted large swathes of free land in North Dakota and elsewhere in the west to anyone willing to settle on it. Prior to that, there was the fur trade boom that made a fortune for, among others, John Jacob Astor, a man who left his mark on New York City by harvesting beaver pelts out here.

It's a peculiarity of the "out here" that it necessitates a "back there." "Economy" has often meant an umbilicus that delivers materials, and the wealth they create, from the former to the latter. There's a lesson here about the ways Americans view the land, even—complicitly—those who live on it, as opposed to those who live on or near the oceans. The land is here to be used. We bristle at fallow fields, idle farms, wild spaces. As accurate as the map in Lynn's office may be, at least in outline, there persists in its outsized rendering something of the *Terra Incognita* of earlier maps. The longer I talk with her—she brightens as we discuss her kids—the more it looks to me like an invitation. *Come West, Young Men. Come West and Seek Your Fortune.*

I understand the anger she feels, but it's hard to blame the refugees—hard even, though I hate to say it, to blame the oil companies. The economy is just this kind of home. It demands you surrender to its imperatives. The fact that there is oil—and money to be made off the money it makes—is enough for people to pack up and move here. To pursue it as one might gold, or sex. The lure is just too powerful to resist. This could be what the surly night clerk at the hotel means when he says the oil boom has to do with gender: the phallus of the drill, the hard-to-get riches.

*

A Few Faces:

Cam's: grizzled, reddened.

The round, pierced faces (lip and nose respectively), lined with long straight hair, of the slightly overweight women at the Hertz counter.

The puckered, sour face of the night clerk, a fatter version of the actor William H. Macy.

The thick blonde mustache lining the upper lip of the man leaning over his biscuits and gravy.

Ben's bright Chippewa face, his stringy black hair worn stylishly mop-top.

The alternately shorn and stubbly faces of the younger workers in their alternately clean and dirty Carhartts.

The scraggly black beard of the young guy in the Lynyrd Skynyrd t-shirt, who looks like he belongs at a Phish concert.

The tweaked out eyes on the pimply face of the burrito bar worker.

Lynn's, framed by her greying blonde hair, both pretty and tired.

*

The workers in the visitor's center, North Dakota enthusiasts in their early fifties, point out that the view from the rotunda is pretty much what things looked like prior to human habitation—if you ignore the mounds from the gravel pits on the horizon. I've come to walk the trails (some groomed, some paved) at the confluence of the Missouri and the Yellowstone. The plains stretch out as plains do, and the rivers meander into one another. There are gentle bluffs and a few steep ones, cottonwoods and native grasses, migrating birds moving from the trees to the ground and back. I linger in the wide, western light, bright enough I feel my face getting red.

The following day, a drizzly Sunday morning, I drive thirty miles north to Lake Zahl, having confirmed with the Fish and Wildlife Service in Crosby that I can walk the grounds. North of the highway is better than south, a man named Monty tells me, and when I arrive I immediately see why. There are hills to the north from which to take in the expanse of the site. Large flocks of migrating waterfowl—I'm too far away and too much of a novice to say what species—float on the many lakes that dot the preserve, one of which must be Lake Zahl. Even here the horizon is dotted with gravel pits and drilling rigs, and the sounds of truck traffic carry over the prairie.

I snap a few photos with my phone, but I can see how insufficient it is to the task. The prairie involves a scale that is almost impossible to reduce to a two-dimensional image, but it also presents a sensory texture—wind rustling the tall grasses, the short ones crunching under your feet—that isn't reproducible. I sit down on a hill facing northwest, and for a moment, sheltered by the plants that surround me, I almost forget what century I'm in. I remember, pathetically, Kevin Costner in *Dances with Wolves*, but it's something of his character's encounter with the vastness of the land that comes to me now. It's as though—again, just for a moment—I've left my cynicism back in the car. I've no sooner had the thought than I receive a text from my wife in Pennsylvania. We're never not part of the world, never disconnected from it—even when we're miles from anything. Costner's character is part and parcel of the expansionism he resists, and my fleeting tranquility here on the hill at Lake Zahl is likewise inseparable from the mania surrounding it.

Drill, baby. Drill.

*

In the Bakken oil fields, as elsewhere, the prospects are collectively known as *the play*, and especially for those involved at the highest levels, a map of North Dakota must look a bit like a Monopoly board. The objects are the same: accumulation, rout. That most of the winners and losers are playing at subsistence levels does not, however, compare all that favorably to the rarefied world of the oil magnate, who has nonetheless managed to idealize his pursuit and to sublimate his rapacity into the dreams of "the common man." Thus, a worker like Cam might wholly identify with the economic aims of his overseers, who are skilled at the appearance of reciprocity. But fortunes are mostly made on the backs of others, and if North Dakota is a Monopoly board, the Cams who move across it in their duallies are, at best, so many top hats and thimbles. The hands that move them are invisible enough they appear to be clean.

Though it may be play for some—unless this too is an attempt at diffusing ideology into everyday life—nobody on the ground is having much fun. Any sense of recreation or of make-believe doesn't apply here, except at a remove. Somebody may be enjoying himself, but it isn't one of the bleary roughnecks or the harried Walmart clerks ringing up carts of Hungry Man dinners. There is about their activity, and the town as a whole, a touch of frenzy and desperation. And unlike children's play, missteps here have consequences. During the three days I'm in town, two deaths are reported: the first is the welder from Alabama, the second is a fifty-five-year-old truck driver from Arizona struck by a train in nearby Ray.

Considering the whole thing as a form of theater doesn't make matters any cheerier. It's hard to see a happy ending, hard to see *any* ending, really, as Williston is the continuation of a larger tragedy by different means, a long-running performance that predates the country's founding and which may outlast any imaginable demise. The extremes of American experience present themselves plainly here, or rather the place stages these extremes, thereby making visible in Williston what is invisible elsewhere: the exceptionalism that insists on conquering the world and remaking it in one's image, so as to redeem it, or us.

Whether or not the Bakken will go bust, as every boom eventually does, is therefore *almost* irrelevant. On one hand, it's useless to bemoan the boom, as it is by now a fait accompli. Even when the bottom falls out on oil prices, as it does just two months after I visit, this particular boulder only gathers momentum as it tumbles down the mountainside. If it hadn't rolled into western North Dakota, it would have done so—is undoubtedly doing so regardless—somewhere else. The problem of Williston isn't actually the problem of Williston at all.

*

On Amerigo Vespucci Discovering America

> "The economy allegorized in Van der Straet's erotic encounter is, of course, much more than simply sexual. Embedded in this gendered exchange are cultural values that privilege the European male's posture in contrast to the Indian female's, which is altogether too receptive, open, and empty, despite her undeniably desirable beauty, which is enhanced by the pastoral gardenlike setting."

Margarita Zamora, on Jan Van der Straet's
16th century illustration, "Discovery of America"

*

Things must get pretty lively at the craft fair in Minot because the administrator at the local art center doesn't show up early as promised, and I have to come back when the doors open at their usual time. For the half hour I spend in the former library, built in memory of the mining and railroad tycoon for whom the town is named, Daniel Willis James, I am the only visitor. Two local girls, *Williston High School National Honor Society* emblazoned on their sweatshirts, direct me to sign the guest register but are otherwise unhelpful, giggling at each other and looking alternately into their textbooks and cellphones.

The exhibit is a series of fifty-three paintings, one for every county in North Dakota. Each pictures a fictional local woman of the sort the artist, Shelly Bunde, says she's known all her life. Highly competent and successful women who work, raise children and grandchildren, produce cookbooks and crafts, and found clubs in their spare time, all while ministering to their husbands and navigating the vicissitudes of a hardscrabble agrarian economy. Each of the images is accompanied by a cut-out of the county in question, culled from a gas station road map, and many include other collaged elements, such as this recipe for a "Busy Day Hot Dish":

1½ C. uncooked macaroni
1 can cream of chicken or mushroom soup
1 can whole kernel corn—drain and add enough milk to make 2 C.
1 can tuna fish
400° 1 hour

The paintings also contain short descriptions of the women, e.g.: "This is Dale Iverson's grand-daughter from Stanley, North Dakota. Her hope chest is only half-full." Or my favorite, glossing the image of a woman holding jumper cables and wrapped in a long winter coat: "Mrs. Steve Lundby of St. Thomas, North Dakota. She feels that there is a bird in her chest that wants to fly. Maybe next spring."

"Growing up in North Dakota in the 1970s," Bunde writes in her "Artist Statement," "I was unaware of the Women's Movement," and consequently in the paintings "every woman or girl but one is identified by her husband's, grandfather's, father's or even father-in-law's name." There was self-effacement (willing and unwilling) in this mostly bygone form of address, Bunde suggests, but "there was more to the women in my town than was apparent." It's this modesty—to the point, sometimes, of servility—that suffuses the paintings with their wryness and melancholy, their simultaneous caricature of and nostalgia for a world that's quickly disappearing. That the Honor Society girls whispering at the table either don't notice or don't care may be part of Bunde's point. The break with the past, in whom it continues, isn't subtle. But while the boom would seem to render the paintings irrelevant—what use does a roughneck have for art?—standing in the large room, once filled with books, it occurs to me the opposite may be true. It's art, and its necessity, that never goes bust.

*

Dear Mary

> The *business* in your periodical's title might justifiably be changed to *politics*, or better yet, *Volksaufklärung*. If I believed you, your writers, or your editorial team possessed the capacity for shame, I might encourage you to feel some.

> May some benevolent god exist, and may she have mercy on your souls.

> Sincerely yours,
> Etc.

*

By the time Sunday evening rolls around I'm ready to get the fuck out. But after I drop off my car at the airport—more of a bus station really, with large gravel parking lots jammed with pickup trucks—there's time for one last pilgrimage to Walmart, which is busy enough that all twenty-five or so checkout lanes are not only open, but each has a small line. Another of the commonplaces about Williston is that the store starts its employees at more than $17 an hour, which isn't nearly as great as it sounds, considering that a three-bedroom apartment, like the one Cam's company rents for him and two other workers, can cost around $3500 a month. Home values have also inflated. Ben purchased his house for $70,000 some years before the boom; it's now worth nearly $400,000. Hard to imagine someone paying that much for it, he admits—it's a basic, one-story affair—but were he to put it on the market he would have no trouble finding a buyer.

Walking through the row of hotels between the airport and the superstore, I pass another landmark of the boom, as reported in the *New York Times*: Boomtown Babes Espresso, a pink shed in front of the Grand Williston Hotel and Conference Center (a squat but sprawling brick building, more ordinary than impressive), popular for its busty, scantily clad baristas. Its competitor, C Cups Espresso, is down the street, behind Home of Economy. It's true that you can practically smell the testosterone in the air here, but that doesn't make this combination of strip club and coffee bar any less surreal. (In Williston these contradictions abound: tomorrow the city will host former vice presidential candidate Sarah Palin, the theme of whose speech, according to the *Herald*, will be the oil industry and Christian education.)

No one may know how the rumors of rapes in the Walmart aisles started, but an atmosphere of sexual predation permeates the civic fabric. Just this morning I read about a man, not a local, currently on trial in Williston for human trafficking, having kidnapped and injected with methamphetamine a Jane Doe at a bar in Stanley, halfway between Williston and Minot. Today at least, the aisles are packed enough that while it's possible to imagine a proposition taking place, even the arguably justifiable (considering the context) crime of shoplifting would be unthinkable. Sunday in Walmart is a sight to see. A holy Sabbath, indeed.

Back in the airport an hour later, I make my way to the double-wide-cum-concourse, where the barred windows are open and the gate agent doesn't need a PA but rather speaks slightly louder than normal to the passengers seated in front of her podium. I board the plane and, as we climb to cruising altitude, Williston disappears beneath the cloud cover. I open my Perec, but my eyes are drawn to the tray table next to me, where a young woman is sketching her apparent avatar, seated with her arms around her knees. The figure's hair is large and frizzy, and something like a dust cloud, or a storm of thoughts, swirls above it.

I've never seen anyone drawing on a plane, I tell her. We chat a little as we eat our peanuts, drink our drinks—water for me, cranberry juice for her. She's been in Watford, another oil town south of Williston, visiting her boyfriend, who has been working out here the past few months—in equipment rental, I gather. He plans to stay until May, when the two of them hope to relocate to San Diego. Meanwhile, she's going home to Grand Rapids, where she's living with her parents and studying business at the community college.

When she shrugs off my suggestion, as though it were below contempt, to pursue her art instead, she immediately epitomizes, in a way that's both endearing and heartrending, those drawn to the Bakken. And I realize what I suspect she already has, if not consciously then intuitively: it's the unlikeliness of her plans coming to fruition—*see you in San Diego!*—that gives her sketching such power. I turn back to my reading, she to her drawing. It's a short flight to Minneapolis, just an hour and a half, and when we land we do not linger in our seats. We do not say goodbye.

Welcome to the heartbeat of America.

THE RISE OF SLIME

*I remember my green extensions, my catfish nuzzlings and minnow
wrigglings, my gelatinous materializations out of the mother ooze.*

Loren Eiseley

It is June and I write to a man I've never met, an eminent zoologist at the
Smithsonian. I'm not a journalist, I tell him. My questions are of another
sort. I wonder whether, as oceanographer Jeremy Jackson claims, we are
living through "the rise of slime," a return to conditions that prevailed in
the primordial oceans, before the evolution of fish. And I wonder whether
jellies are part and parcel of this rise, weedy generalists who might be
considered, according to one Australian researcher, the cockroaches of the
sea. I ask if I can come visit. Poke around and ask questions. I don't say I
traffic in metaphor. It doesn't feel necessary or relevant in this early phase,
and I worry that I might come across as a crank, chasing crackpot ideas
into his lab.

Soon it's mid-July and I'm waiting at 10th and Constitution, outside
the north entrance to the museum. It's a Friday morning and there's a line
of preschoolers in matching yellow shirts, each connected by a long rope.
Italians and Germans wait in the vestibule and an officious guard directs
traffic. It is not yet oppressively warm, as it will be when I leave the building
that afternoon, but there is already a slight swelter in the air. The zoologist,
Allen Collins, arrives just after ten in a bright yellow hat, easy to spot in
the busy summer crowd. He is an immediately likeable, athletic man in his
late forties, with two young children he has just shuttled to soccer camp.
He leads me through a bewildering series of stairwells and back hallways
to a newly established lab for culturing jellies, which is where we find
his summer intern, a bright student at a prestigious high school near

DC. They're having some trouble with one or two trays of polyps that don't appear to be growing, but she manages to find one for me under the microscope. It's an unfortunate reality of the work I do, I say, squinting at a tubular structure I have difficulty describing, that there aren't many petri dishes in my life.

We chat with the intern in the windowless room, which is little more, Collins admits, than a closet, but his goal is to have some live animals on display, especially now that the invertebrate house at the National Zoo is closing down. Outreach is increasingly a priority for the scientists, Collins says, and to his credit he appears to like it. He tells me that when he recently set up a microscope on a dock in Bali to show the locals plankton, they were incredulous: did he mean to tell them the plankton were both invisible and all around? Still, I sense his hesitation: the outreach is not the work, and there's some danger (professionally, if nothing else) in letting it take over. The longer you spend with the public, the less time you spend in the lab.

We walk to a crowded office full of specimen jars. The formalin keeps them together, he says, but, shaking one ever so slightly, some flesh flakes off nonetheless. We talk for some time in front of a poster displaying the cnidarian tree of life, a project with which he was intimately involved. He wasn't always a scientist, he says. In college he studied math and economics before beginning a career in business. He planned on getting an MBA, applied and was accepted into some good schools. Then, just for fun, he took a course on the history of the earth and something shifted. He delayed his MBA admission and in the meantime continued taking night courses in biology and paleontology. By the end of the year he was hooked, and his plans changed accordingly. We think life moves in a linear fashion, he says, but it's more like a flow chart. There are so many variables, potential routes one might take. Chance plays a part, as does luck.

"In motion, jellies mesmerize us," I read months earlier, on a placard at the Shedd Aquarium in Chicago, where a temporary exhibit on jellies had been extended for years because of the enormous public response. The room was dark and ambient new age music streamed through hidden speakers. I watched a young lion's mane jelly move forward by almost turning itself inside out. "Beautiful," another placard asked, "or too much of a good thing?" As the long, stringy tentacles tangled with one another, almost as though in knots, I thought that the question only hinted at the ironies it contained, which linked beauty to waste and pleasure to ruin.

I saw a boy rushing from one display to the next, tugging on his father's arm. I identified with them both, the hurried and the harried, and in another way with the teenage girl who pointed out a comb jelly to her friends, calling it a rainbow jelly instead, in keeping with the shimmering of its waving cilia. The exhibit boasted a video game in which players capture various forms of pollution (fertilizer, spilled oil, plastic trash) to prevent the formation of a dead zone, which is the semi-technical (and, I would later learn, misleading) term for the proliferating hypoxic regions in the world's oceans where *some* jellies are flourishing. I played the game poorly, both amused and dismayed by the necessity of the interactive gimmick, from which I learned more about the changing nature of museums than about the factors that contribute to so-called jelly blooms, although the game, in that it turned disaster into sport, may have been instructive when it came to that as well.

As for the jellies, there was something otherworldly in how slowly they moved, pulsing through the water as though extensions of it. In Brazil, jellies are *água-viva*, living water, and as our fetishization of birds may be linked to a longing for flight, our fetishization of jellies may be linked to a longing for return, back to our primordial origins. As birds symbolize hope ("the thing with feathers," as Dickinson famously has it), jellies may symbolize our nostalgia for a gone world, the one embedded in the salinity of our veins. I admired how they drifted across the panes of glass, seemingly passive participants in the currents. Was it that, standing there in the gallery, I envied their acquiescence, their movement that was not exactly motion, or was it that, in all my rushing to and fro, all my self-assertion, there remained some part of me that longed to be carried, to give up on influencing events and be swept away instead?

"For much of its life cycle," I read that day in the aquarium, "a jelly doesn't look like a jelly at all." If this were mere metamorphosis it might be of passing interest, but the reproductive cycle of jellies is arguably stranger than that of butterflies and moths. Some adults live only weeks or months, and fertilization happens largely by chance. Generally speaking, a male releases a cloud of sperm, a female a cloud of eggs, and the currents carry these clouds toward each other. Fertilized eggs become tiny larvae called planulae, which then settle on the ocean floor, where they turn into polyps. These can stay dormant for decades, and they can also divide and multiply. At least in the case of so-called true jellies (or Scyphozoa), they split into stacks of small disks, which break off (the technical term is *strobilation*) to become, eventually, what we recognize as adult jellies. The medusae (i.e., the adult jellies) are genetically identical to the polyps, however, so there's some question not only as to what a jelly looks like, but as to what the organism even is, whether it's the polyp or the medusa or, if both, how peculiar for a thing to be alive in multiple places at once.

We're used to thinking of organisms as individuals, but cnidarians (the phylum of which jellies—and corals, among others—are part) defy that training. They don't invest their energy in singularity so much as multiplicity (or multiplicity as singularity), even though some medusae can reach the length of two school buses. They spread out. They take up space. They can be compared to colonial organisms, as certain species technically are. One cnidarian Collins shows me, called a siphonophore, looks a bit like foxglove: individual bells budding from and along a single stem. These "bells" are zooids, linked organisms that serve different functions, each highly dependent on the others. Seen one way, the zooids are individuals; seen another way, the colony is. The same might be said of jellies in general: the medusae are alternately individuals or parts of a larger, rhizomatic whole. More remarkable yet, because of their endless cloning and reproduction, their long cycles of dormancy and bloom, jellies are almost immortal. Sure, the medusae grow and die (although some can deintegrate themselves and reform planulae from the remaining material), but the polyps persist. A jelly can die in one form and live on in another. I'm not sure I've done, or can do, justice to how exceedingly strange this is.

But then the world is full of rats that laugh and parrots that call each other by name. Our ears just aren't capable of hearing them. With its twenty-four eyes, on the other hand, the box jelly can simultaneously take in detail and atmosphere, but without a brain—or rather, with something like a brain diffused throughout its body—it cannot make the combinations mean. Maybe, as Amy Leach writes, this brainlessness "is a direct consequence of its tremendous powers of sight." "Perhaps," she continues, "neither the animal nor the prophet has been invented who could process so thorough a vision." Or perhaps, I might add, what that processing looks like would be alien to us, as jellies are. Our own brains, rather large relative to our body size, may be the most powerful processing instruments yet developed, but even they may not be effective enough to combine, except in the briefest of instances, the parts and the whole, the moment and the synopsis, the light and the detail. And this could be a lucky thing for us, a defense against annihilation. Leach writes, "it is disquieting enough to be hyperacute *or* hypersensitive; perhaps being both would very soon melt your brain and leave you quiescent, hanging transparently in the giant dancing green waters of the world."

At lunch we are joined by a second zoologist, the director of the marine biology center at the University of São Paulo. He has the distinct, charming cadence to his fluent English that native Portuguese speakers often do. His presence is warm but sober, as a friend of his, a leading figure in the field, has just died. He's curious about what I'm writing, but I say I'm not sure what it will become just yet. I use a jelly analogy and say that my interest has cultured many polyps that have yet to strobilate into full-fledged medusae. When the joke doesn't take, I add that in my early twenties I visited the popular exhibit in Monterey Bay but didn't learn a thing about jellies, except that they were beautiful. I didn't understand that, displayed as they were, they were meant to be, that in visiting the aquarium I was having less of a scientific experience than an aesthetic one, as though proper lighting could hide the fact that this complex of buildings committed to the preservation of marine life had once been dedicated to its eradication.

Beauty is one of the refrains about jellies, and it comes up again in the staff cafeteria. The Brazilian, Antonio Marques, describes an exhibition he's recently read about in the blighted city of Liverpool. Two artists, Walter Hugo and Zoniel, have installed aquaria containing jellies in an abandoned building. They are meant to contrast their dilapidated surroundings, I gather, but considering the recent alarm over the apparent increase in destructive blooms (one infamous Black Sea event measured a thousand fist-sized jellies per cubic yard), this contrast must be ironic at best. Beauty is a cultural category as much as, if not more than, an intrinsic one, and in its application to jellies I sense the old conjunction of the beautiful and the terrible, I say. Given the state of the world's oceans—and here the irony of the exhibit enters in—it doesn't make sense to claim the former for jellies without acknowledging the latter. More to the point, what might otherwise repulse us can be converted, sometimes without much effort, into a source of delight, and jellies are part of that perversity.

Once at a job talk, I tell the zoologists, I said that jellies are creepy. The department chair objected: what's wrong with them? she asked, they're pretty beautiful to me. I said she was right, of course, but that what's creepy about this sludging up of our oceans—Jackson's rise of slime—is that we take pleasure, through expensive aquarium displays, in its products. Beauty would appear to almost excuse our excesses, but this strikes me, I added, as an insidious self-justification.

Jellies aren't repulsive, Marques says—we are. But he's only right insofar as the department chair was. Our repulsion is matched by our fascination, and both are embedded in the language of our descriptions. While they are often framed in aesthetic terms—one Monterey Bay exhibit was entitled *Jellies: Living Art*—they are also framed in the media, even by some scientists, as a "plague," as "slime," as "the cockroaches of the sea." Behind a glass wall, jellies are lovely; at the beach, they're a menace. But our aesthetic categories have reversed the ecological ones, and while evolutionarily the ocean is the "right" place for jellies, our presence has turned it into the "wrong" one. Jellies are beautiful only when they don't impede us; they're repulsive whenever they do. In both cases, we're the dominant factor, the constant in the equation.

The dilemma extends to rats and weeds and coyotes and pigeons, the synanthropes that thrive in the conditions that accompany human dominance—*syn-*, meaning with, or together, or alike, and *-anthrope* deriving from the Greek word for human. A cockroach is thus a *like-human,* or *with-human,* as is a mosquito, though all these creatures could be classified as pests, a word that derives in English from the fifteenth-century French term (*peste*, from the Latin *pestis*) for the bubonic plague. That humans breed pestilence may reflect the planetary affliction we are, or have become—a contagion that insists the world (or parts of it) is beautiful even as, or possibly because, it is ravaged. This may be a misanthropic view, but one grounded in the degree to which we have become wrongly, or perversely, or mistakenly human.

Then again, the current appears to run the other way: from mistakenness to sameness. Jon Mooallem writes that the loss, at the end of the Pleistocene, of big animals like mastodons and smilodons "has meant that, for the last twelve thousand years, every human generation has inherited a North America that is profoundly out of whack." "So many ecosystems we see, study, and appreciate, are," he says, "mostly ruins—a disheveled set of ripple effects, reverberating from the loss of these big and influential beasts." In cannily placing ourselves at the top of the food chain, the rest of the living world has had to either adapt to our ambitions or go the way of the mastodon. It's not that we have eliminated nature, but that we have reshaped it in our image—even if doing so has turned the world into the series of compounding errors (climate change, overfishing, agricultural runoff, among others) that make increasingly large patches of the oceans increasingly hospitable to certain species of jellies.

Marques is right in this way, too: jellies aren't a plague, and to assert their weediness (another cultural category) is inevitably to acknowledge our own. A weed is just doing what it's good at, capitalizing on conditions. Jellies can't be blamed for taking advantage of circumstances conducive to their growth any more than dandelions can be blamed for spreading across a lawn. When it comes to humans, the question is more complicated, Collins suggests: we know better, or should. We have our dignity, Jeremy Jackson says, to uphold. But we're also opportunists, weedy generalists who consume a lot and who aren't, on balance, terribly picky about what we eat and where we live. We exploit the planet *because we can*. And the trouble with being part of the colonial organism called human civilization is that, as with the siphonophores, the intentions of any individual actor are mostly subordinate to the prerogatives of the whole, which are to grow and to survive by any means. Dignity might not enter into it.

For the scientists who study them, the zoologists say, the recent alarm over jellies has raised the question of whether their populations are increasing. Locally and anecdotally it appears that they are, particularly in coastal areas where conditions have degraded into dead zones, which is a misnomer in the sense that these areas are actually teeming with life and abounding in nutrients. It just isn't the "right" life, the one that predominated prior to human intervention. (In this sense, Marques says, the zone is "dead": the previous ecology has disappeared.) And while there are weedy species of cnidarians, Collins tells me these generally belong to two orders of jellies in the subclass Discomedusae: Semaeostomeae and Rhizostomeae. As for "the cockroach of the sea," the analogy just doesn't hold. There are already creatures—a relative of lobsters—that fit the description and have a comparable ecological niche. If you look at a chart of the cnidarian phylum, as we did earlier in the day, the species implicated in blooms are relegated to a small corner. Most cnidarians aren't doing nearly as well, and some (e.g., corals) are even in dramatic decline. Many are poorly understood and rarely studied.

We have finished lunch at this point and are talking in Collins's new office, which is, in contrast to his old one, remarkably spare (the new furniture, he says, has yet to arrive). Both men point me to a study by another scientist, Rob Condon of the University of North Carolina at Wilmington, who claims (along with his co-authors) that we know too little to say definitively what is happening, although it does appear that there's a 20-year boom and bust cycle for jellies. Are blooms happening locally? Undoubtedly. Does this have implications for global populations? Too early to tell, Condon says. Marques calls it a conservative paper that stakes out the limits of what we know and what we don't, refusing to fall in with the overriding mood of alarm. It's good science, he says.

My visit is coming to a close, but I ask about Lise-Ann Gershwin's recent book, *Stung*. Both men know Gershwin, but neither has read the book. The two defend her scientific credentials, which are apparent in the writing, but I wonder if there's a bit of what George Saunders calls the braindead megaphone at work in her rise to prominence—and in the prevailing, sensational message (disseminated by Gershwin, Jackson, and others) that jellies are a terrible, end-times curse we've brought on ourselves. Right now, hers sounds like the loudest voice in the room, and whether or not her position is the most informed, it has the capacity—like a good weed—to crowd out others.

The curious flipside to this comes in the form of another visitor who joins us briefly near the end. His claim about the closing of the invertebrate house is that the Zoo's director, a former Coca-Cola executive, cares more about charismatic megafauna—pandas and elephants—than he does about conservation. He wants to raise money by putting butts in the seats, so to speak, and he believes (our species being what it is) that a baby panda will arouse public interest better than a nautilus. For him spectacle trumps science. It's a different strain of a familiar cynicism. In one version, a certain animal is wrong for the oceans because it hinders human activity (*even if* the former is a product of the latter); in the other, a certain animal is wrong for the zoo because it cannot be monetized. In each instance, the human scale obtains, pairing our self-esteem with our self-loathing.

Before long it's after two and the zoologists have to run to a meeting, but as I'm preparing to leave, Marques pulls up a few prints by the nineteenth-century biologist Ernst Haeckel on his laptop—gorgeous, intricate panels he published under the title *Kustformen der Natur*, or *Art Forms of Nature*. Haeckel featured cnidarians prominently in the collection, including box jellies, sea anemones, hydroids, and siphonophores—many of which he originally named and described. Among the most striking of the highly stylized images is the eighth print in the series, which illustrates three varieties of Discomedusae. Swirling from bottom right to bottom left, then across the image at a diagonal to the upper right, is *Desmonema annasethe,* a species Haeckel described in 1880 and whose tentacles are said to have reminded him of his wife's hair. His images remind me, on the other hand, of the poster I'm holding, a souvenir from a 2013 Italian conference Collins has given me, which features twenty-two glossy jellies against a matte background. That they've been photoshopped, which is to say aestheticized, strikes me as a contemporary extension of Haeckel's compositions, as artistic as they are accurate.

I bid the men goodbye, happy to have spent the day talking jellies, at the entrance to an exhibit on human history funded by one of the notorious Koch brothers. When I finally return to my hotel, late in the afternoon, I'm troubled to read, while looking online for the prints Marques showed me, that among Ernst Haeckel's most prominent claims was that "politics is applied biology," a sentiment avidly embraced by his countrymen in the years between world wars. For Haeckel, the great proponent of nature as art—and a fine aestheticizer of jellies—was also one of the leading lights of scientific racism, and his beliefs helped fuel the fascism that devastated Europe.

As I consider the familiar implications, here in my hotel room just south of the mall, I am reminded of the twenty-four eyes of the box jelly: my inability to separate the marvelous from the monstrous, the scientific from the aesthetic, the reasoned from the arbitrary—or inflammatory—may be, like the jelly's brainlessness, a defense against annihilation. If only I could make these combinations mean, but then to do so may be to condemn the whole human endeavor. And misanthropy occludes, offers no way out or through or forward. I remember what Collins said at the start of my visit, in connection to his early corporate aspirations, that life is less about cause and effect than chance and luck and complexity. I'm bumping up against the mind's limits here, trying both to describe the flowchart and be swept away by it. Much as pleasure may be ruin and ruin pleasure, beauty may be waste and waste beauty, but as for what holds such contrarieties together, it's slime—glorious, gooey, and human.

FLUTTER POINT

THE SUM OF TWO CUBES (AND THE USES OF LITERATURE)

1.

In January of 1913, a twenty-five-year-old autodidact by the name of Srinivasa Ramanujan wrote a letter to the British mathematician G.H. Hardy. He had already written to a number of prominent academics, but Hardy would be the only one to respond. A little more than a year later Ramanujan boarded a ship in Madras bound for London. Soon he was in Cambridge, where, even as his health deteriorated (in part because of the weather, in part because of the food), he collaborated with Hardy and lived out the duration of the First World War.

Hardy had recognized Ramanujan's brilliance almost immediately. His approach was highly intuitive, notable in a field dominated by logical demands. But his thinking also had its blindspots. As Hardy once said of him, "The limitations of his knowledge were as startling as its profundity." Even though Hardy wondered what Ramanujan would have been capable of had he enjoyed the same privileges, part of the beauty of Ramanujan's story is that he was not limited by the knowledge out of which men like Hardy made careers.

Having a relatively poor mind for math myself, my interest in Ramanujan has less to do with his research on Bernoulli numbers than with the fact that, at the conclusion of the war and in terrible health, he returned to India, where, having left a definitive mark on modern mathematics, he died at the age of thirty-three.

2.

But you will forgive me, Comrades. I have overshot my mark. I have not begun at the beginning. Let me retrace my steps and begin again.

First, let it be assumed that everywhere we touch the world meaning proliferates, and that this fecundity is what makes the dual activities of reading and writing so pleasurable. Let it also be assumed that this pleasure can, as an unintended consequence, produce *paranoia*, by which I mean both the commonly implied delirium and something else entirely. The word comes from the Greek root *nous*, meaning mind, and the prefix *para-* (as in *paradox*, *paraphrase*, and *paradise*) meaning "analogous or parallel to" but also "beyond." I am interested, here, in appraising a mind that is like mind, separate from or just beyond it. A mind untethered to mind. What language would such a mind speak? I want to describe a position from which thinking can address the world, but buoyantly, as though thought could suspend us above the melee of daily life.

I also want to examine where writing leads us, and how it takes us there. Although literature may not be an entirely useless endeavor, it comes pretty damn close sometimes. The fact that everything can be found to have some use, however provisional, does not mean that those phenomena nearest to uselessness on an imaginary spectrum are, to all intents and purposes, useful. In a house, one wants every square foot to be accounted for, to have some purpose. In my own house, we have even found a use for the space beneath the stairs. But while much domestic architecture may abhor impracticality, in literature it may be cause for celebration.

Useful or no, let us assume that any product of a culture is inseparable from the conditions that produce it. What to make of the fact, then, that one of the most radical of American art forms—abstract expressionist painting—was secretly supported by the CIA, and that many of the most lauded names in twentieth-century American art were unwitting weapons in an artistic cold war conducted alongside the actual one? Such an extreme case may be beside the point, but to say that my writing exists in a world separate from and untouched by Lady Gaga's meat dress, on one hand, and, on the other, the ongoing horrors in the eastern Congo, is to claim for art a privilege that is at once self-congratulatory and self-deceptive. I have almost no interest in a programmatic or didactic art, but the buoyant position I am imagining is also not insouciance. The work I have in mind, the stance I want to champion, is never exempt from the realities it addresses or fails to address.

3.

In our public library, the one I go to with my family, there are several versions of the story of the pied piper available in the children's section. I find the story horrifying, and leafing through some pages this past week I was struck by the fact that the faces of the children, as they are being led out of town, are bright and cheerful. Like the piper, the children are dancing down the street, across the bridge, and into the countryside beyond. Their happiness would be obscene if they knew any better, but under the spell of the piper's flute they don't.

One widely reproduced photograph from 9/11 shows a group of people chatting along the Brooklyn waterfront, apparently unbothered by the smoking buildings in the background. The image, as was subsequently revealed, is more complex than that (one of the pictured, Walter Sipser, claims the group was in "a profound state of shock and disbelief"), but there is also the unrelated photograph of beachgoers outside Naples soaking up the sun while the bodies of two drowned teenage girls—whom nobody bothered to save—lie in open sight some ten feet away. Indifference, yes, and one could certainly write about the social, psychological, and artistic dimensions of that indifference. My interest, though, is in a lightness that acknowledges the bodies on the beach or the burning buildings by barely acknowledging them at all.

As elsewhere, one of my guides here is W. G. Sebald, who performed this task with a relentlessness that is as stunning as it is deeply sad. The unnamed subject of each of Sebald's books is, by his own admission, the concentration camps, but, with a few exceptions, he touches on them so lightly that you could be lulled by his long, languorous sentences into thinking the books were about something else: herring, say, or the rise of the Dowager Empress. That they are not, or not fully, is a function of a Sebaldian principle: atrocity requires no exaggeration. If you look closely you see how it saturates all that surrounds it, drawing the energy of the world into its deep and abhorrent abyss. But lightness, in Sebald and elsewhere, provides more than a cover. Lightness is a strategy, much as I distrust that word. It is a method for dealing with and channeling other energies.

A single memo at the end of Georges Perec's *Species of Spaces*, an incomparably light text, illustrates what I mean. The memo describes a landscaping project to be completed outside of the crematorium ovens at Auschwitz; the correspondents are two of the camp's administrators. This is likely the exact place where Perec's own mother was murdered. So why include the letter? What practical use could it serve? It is typical of the method I have in mind that the lightness here is heavy-light, much as Coleridge argued for the virtues of the clear-obscure. In the case of *Species of Spaces*, what the letter represents is heavy enough that it could sink any text that included it, which is also why Perec says nothing whatsoever about it. But the opposite is equally important: without some counterbalance, the purely light text drifts off like a loose balloon. Montaigne writes: "Let the mind awaken and quicken the heaviness of the body: let the body arrest the lightness of the mind and fix it fast." Meanwhile the balloon floats higher and higher. I can see it now, there above the plains. It's pretty, yes, but I can't hold it. It's pretty, yes, but it won't last.

4.

In 1940, G.H. Hardy published a famous book-length essay, *A Mathematician's Apology*. Hardy begins his work with the melancholy admission that "Exposition, criticism, appreciation is work for second-rate minds"—melancholy because this is precisely what Hardy is undertaking. The book is premised on the painful realization that his creative period as a mathematician is over and now all that's left to him is to reflect on what it has meant.

In his *Apology*, Hardy opposes what he calls real with trivial mathematics and argues that while the latter is, on the whole, useful, "real [or pure] mathematics does not, 'do good' in a certain sense." Real mathematics, he says, has no effect on war. Trivial mathematics, on the other hand, can be applied to a wide variety of combat scenarios. Mathematics can be used to plot the trajectory of a missile, but the study of pure mathematics generally has no comparable application. (While it's curious to note that Hardy's particular field of study has since been applied to cryptology, I recently spoke with a "pure" mathematician who assured me that 99% of what he does is as useless as number theory was in Hardy's time.)

Hardy concludes by saying that he has never done anything useful, anything "likely to make, directly or indirectly, for good or ill, the least difference to the amenity of the world." W.H. Auden's axiom that "Poetry makes nothing happen" reminds me that, as writers, we may find ourselves in a similar situation. The phrase I often heard repeated at Naropa—that poetry propels the century forward a few inches—is only a slight revision of Auden's phrase, since, given the severity of our situation as a species (overpopulation, climate change, global poverty) the difference between nothing and a few inches may be piddling.

The writer Maggie Nelson has written her own revision of Auden, but with a slight twist. Writing, she says in her marvelously troubling book *Bluets*, changes nothing. Like fucking, it leaves everything pretty much the way it is. Fucking happens because, on a biological level, we have to fuck. We're hardwired that way. Is writing any less biologically determined? Do we write because we have to write? (And among American writers, to paraphrase Frank O'Hara, which ones are better than fucking?) How conscious of a decision, for a writer, is the one to write? Like fucking, it must be slightly more conscious than breathing, but less conscious than choosing what to order (A burger? A salad?) for lunch.

Writing is not unlike what producing mathematical proofs was for Hardy, or better yet Ramanujan. Did I mention that Ramanujan's stay in England was exactly contemporaneous with the First World War? Did I mention that Hardy's *Apology* was undertaken in 1939, in the deep crease of the Second? That its composition came only after the heart attack that same year that left him as incapable of playing real tennis as conducting real math?

5.

According to Italo Calvino, lightness is one of the supreme virtues of literature, and by lightness he means something that loosens objects from their inevitable heaviness, a "weightless gravity" in which the world is suspended. Privations produce a desire for levitation, he writes, and it is precisely this need to hover above or beyond the surface of our reality that literature enables.

There are a couple of ways to read this, the first of which has a distinctly escapist edge. In short, to banish actual privation from one's writing and to adopt, instead, the fantasies literature allows: ordered worlds, clear justice, happy endings. There are plenty of literary examples of this in both realist novels and fantasy fiction: the world of the sitcom, even when cloaked in distinctly darker tones. The second possibility is something like Hamlet's melancholy, which Calvino describes not as a "dense, opaque" sadness, "but a veil of minute particles of humours and sensations, a fine dust of atoms." Veils must be remarkably light (although having never worn one, I can't say with any certainty), but functionally speaking a veil does not reinvent the world but filters and distorts it. A veil destabilizes the wearer's relationship to objects, and vice versa. Through one, reality isn't absent: it's just fuzzy.

The hero Perseus, Calvino writes, kills the gorgon Medusa by viewing her reflection in the polished surface of his shield. You may never find a lighter story about a beheading than this one, but the act is still grisly. Sure, it's a fantastic horror, but it's a horror nonetheless. And within it are the seeds of the sadism and misogyny that have dominated much of human history. Calvino's point, however, is that Perseus only succeeds in overcoming the terrible beauty of the gorgon by approaching it indirectly. In Perseus's hands lightness is not the opposite of weight but something like its casing or shell. Or, to reverse the formulation, weight is not the opposite of lightness but its lining.

Calvino insists that such lightness is not the abolition of reality. Perseus, he says, does not refuse "the reality in which he is fated to live; he carries the reality with him and accepts it as his particular burden." His challenge, like the writer's, is not to get bogged down by "the weight, the inertia, the opacity of the world"; rather, it's to address that weight without succumbing to it. There's an equal but opposite risk, however: veils with nothing on the other side of them, shields in which no Gorgon lurks and where the image is instead, and narcissistically, one's own. What's offensive about the lightness present in many of our cultural products is not offensive to any sense of propriety, but to the world itself.

Nor is it elitist to say so. Our culture retains a deep distrust of intellect and nurtures a nearly paralyzing fear of what it does not understand. That many readers still find Gertrude Stein opaque, for example, may have less to do with Stein's approach to language and reality than with our failure, albeit over several generations, to incorporate her challenge to language into everyday life. Difficulty is not to be avoided. As Chögyam Trungpa often said, we need to lean into the sharp points. Not impale ourselves, but not run away either.

6.

A few years ago, I went to see a gifted body-worker. She spent a generous amount of time working on me, probably two hours, but only one thing stands out in my memory: the single, extraordinarily light touch at the site of an injury I had sustained months before. It's possible she didn't even touch the site, but much of my body's energy was clearly pooling itself there. All it required was the slightest gesture to be released into the air. The experience was electric. I shuddered. It was deeply moving, even though it only lasted a second or two. More remarkable yet, while she was aware of my injury and its general location, I don't remember saying exactly where it was. I didn't need to. All of us wear our wounds far more openly than we suppose. For those who know how to look, they mark us all too clearly.

A skilled body-worker herself, Bhanu Kapil performs something similar in her recent book, *Schizophrene*. The work contains its share of violence, including an assault, a race riot, and a scene from post-partition India in which the writer's young mother catches a glimpse of a row of women tied to trees along the new border, their stomachs cut out. Kapil doesn't dwell on this violence, giving us little context. As a result the touch, despite the heaviness of the situations she describes, feels light and even—although I hesitate to say it—electric. The best example in the book may be a single page that reads, in quotation marks, "He dragged her down the stairs by her hair to the room where we were eating." That's it. Nothing more. We don't learn the pronouns' referents, we don't know who the speaker is, and the context of both the act and the statement are purposefully withheld. All that remains is the horror, alone on the page, and then we move on. We have touched the site of the injury and that is sufficient. In witnessing, we have validated.

But to what end? The intention here can hardly be to stop domestic violence, even if one is fundamentally committed to that goal. Am I saying what is already obvious to everyone? That the writer's personal and social commitments are inseparable from her work and also incommensurable with it? So why write a scene of such violence into a work unlikely to have much of an effect on the continuation of that violence? For me, and I suspect for Kapil as well, the answer always comes back to the body and to the necessity of writing and living from the curious mixture, I might call it the hybridity, at one's core. If writing is indeed a biological imperative, if literature is as much a physical construct as a social one, how can the body of the text avoid reflecting the body of the person who produced it? And if this body, any body, is present when "He drag[s] her down the stairs by her hair to the room where we [a]re eating," to deny expression to that memory, felt in the scalp, would be as painful and as pointless as exaggerating it.

7.

Hardy argues that his work—real or pure mathematics—is indefensible from certain moral positions. Literature, he suggests, if it's of any permanent value, is equally indefensible. How can you defend your decision to study literature when about half of the world's population lives on around $2 a day? If you have never seen what $2 a day looks like, you'll have to take my word for it when I say that the scale on which life is lived in this way is a sin so great that I know of no word in any language to name it. Considering that literature is unlikely to ameliorate that poverty, where does its value reside? What are its uses? Is the most that can be said for it that it is harmless? And can't this harmlessness be construed as an ethical lapse?

A case could be made for the text as a devotional object—the *rite* within *write*—and it bears mentioning that Ramanujan (have we forgotten about him?) was apparently a deeply religious man. Hardy was an atheist (how could he not have been?) but his writings on the aesthetics of pure mathematics strike a distinctly mystical tone. As the battle of the Somme raged in Europe, claiming more than a million lives in just five months, these two men were writing papers on the qualities of integers. Like high priests in some hidden temple, albeit a secular one named Cambridge University, they reverently performed their duties while the world around them went to the dogs.

But why?

Hardy writes, "When the world is mad, a mathematician may find in mathematics an incomparable anodyne." Not a cure, mind you, but something like a painkiller. Such an anodyne might also take the form of a light touch at or near the spot along the right eye socket where the nose meets the forehead. It might even take the form of a book—Kapil's *Schizophrene*, say. The question her book begs, after all, is whether writing also can serve as a balm. Can it heal? Or does it, at most, speak to the body's need for healing? Does it suggest the balm it cannot itself provide?

8.

During the war it was difficult for Ramanujan to leave England, and, to make matters worse, before his departure he was even hospitalized for a time. Hardy would often come to visit, and one day he found himself considering the number of the taxi he was riding in, 1729. Once at Ramanujan's bedside, Hardy said the number struck him as quite uninteresting, mathematically speaking. Ramanujan protested: it was the lowest number that could be expressed as the sum of two cubes in two different ways. The mind that could grasp this complexity instantaneously is so foreign to me as to induce naïve awe, but that Ramanujan's apprehension was both profound and profoundly useless may be what I find so moving about the anecdote.

Hardy insists that it's wrong to talk about the usefulness of pure mathematics or art, since there is practically no use for either. The best he can come up with is that he pushed the century forward a few inches, adding a small portion to the sum of human knowledge. Say what you will, Hardy tells us, I collaborated with the best minds of my generation as something like a peer. Still, one can't help feeling that Hardy sees his life as a failure, especially as he grasps that his best powers as a mathematician have left him. It could have been this that led Hardy, at the end of the Second World War, to attempt suicide. Unfortunately, as he told his friend C.P. Snow, he found he had no aptitude for it and took far more pills than necessary. Then again, he could have been driven to self-destruction by his inability to justify a life spent playing, albeit with numbers, while a massive orgy of violence claimed, all told, tens of millions of lives. Inevitably, the question with which he begins his *Apology*, that of the ultimate value of his work, remains unanswered and, at least by Hardy, unanswerable. (One can reasonably assume that Hardy would roll in his grave if he knew his work was being vulgarized in every credit card transaction that takes place.)

In his memoir *Fugitive Days*, former Weather Underground member Bill Ayers recounts his first contacts with leading figures in the anti-war movement and in Students for a Democratic Society (SDS). He remembers the early rallying cry: try to live in a way that does not make a mockery of your values. This exhortation also haunts Hardy's *Apology*, and is the real source of the book's melancholy. Tempted as I am to revise that earlier catchphrase into *write in a way that does not make a mockery of your values*, I don't know whether our work can ever align precisely with our values, though I'm also not saying we shouldn't try.

9.

A light touch does not negate reality, nor are all silences complicit. Anne Carson, in her moving elegy for her brother, *Nox*, talks about a muteness or opacity "which likes to show the truth by allowing it to be seen hiding." And near the end of *Schizophrene*, Bhanu Kapil includes a page that has been totally blacked out. The opaque square of ink defies you to see through it, or to place words on the page. There is some truth here, or some horror, that is inaccessible to us—something we are not allowed to see but are allowed to see hiding. The page has a famous precedent: in Laurence Sterne's *Tristram Shandy*, a black page appears after the death of one of the characters. As in Sterne's famous book, the effect of Kapil's page is not, paradoxically, a sense of heaviness. Or at least, not a sense of heaviness alone: some weight has been lifted and this one page, of all the pages in the book, is allowed to levitate, to unhinge the book from its subject. It accomplishes this through a lightness so dark it's opaque, through ink so dense it's mute.

10.

Someone who makes a living writing ad copy or political speeches or satire might argue—as would certain champions of the Virtues of Literature— that language has a profound capacity to shape who we are, how we think, what we buy. I agree. Wholeheartedly. And yet I also suspect that those black pages in *Schizophrene* and *Tristram Shandy* are the purest form of literature there is, even if it's an impossible and undesirable ideal.

Language as tool, language as literature: the two may occasionally overlap, but it's unlikely any literary work will change your life in the way that an instruction manual will teach you how to run your new microwave. Whatever use there is to literature has nothing to do with such efficacy. Instrumental language reduces possibility—push this button—but when literary language touches the world, meaning proliferates.

Like Hardy before me, I may be leaving you with a melancholy picture. I wanted to say something about writing, about usefulness not correlating with beauty. But I'm less concerned, at the end of these notes, with writing and mathematics, Ramanujan and Hardy, Calvino and Kapil. I've even forgotten the words to the Radiohead song about the pied piper that inspired me to begin this piece, a song I haven't listened to in years but which I remember moving me through its muteness.

Instead, I am thinking of a brittle ring of sand in Papua New Guinea, the highest point of which is no more than a meter above sea level at high tide. Five hundred people call Takuu home, but the island, says the writer and cartographer Judith Schalansky, is sinking. The beach narrows with every storm. Pieces of land often disappear overnight. The older inhabitants refuse to admit what is happening. They build dykes. They pray. The young people, though more realistic about their prospects, are no more useful than the rocks and brushwood bundled in nets and cast on the shore. All day long, they "drink the juice of the coconut palm, fermented in the hot sunlight," and though it isn't the way I spend my days, here at my end of the world, I wonder whether, given a taste of that juice, it could be.

1. Stating the Question

A few years ago I was having dinner with a writer who, between bites of his steak, connected his reading of Viktor Shklovsky to the chairs at our table. Shklovsky had been a revelation, he said, because he no longer had to discuss what a text meant; he could focus instead on how it had been made. Didn't that drain reading of a certain pleasure? I asked. He pointed to the chair I was sitting on: what did I care what the chair meant? The only thing that mattered was whether the chair worked. Could I sit on it? Was it comfortable?

I have a question about beauty that begins at IKEA, though it hardly ends there. Maybe it's better to say I'm curious about what kind of beauty is available to someone who shops at IKEA, what kind of beauty—if that's the right word—a shopper seeks from the store. Is it fair, I wonder, to call this beauty cheap? Meretricious? This isn't precisely my question.

I don't intend to denounce the big blue store. It has free daycare, a cheap restaurant, and its showroom is a bit like a corn maze. You can spend hours getting lost on a rainy day for nothing more than the cost of a meal—and that's only if you get hungry. More to the point, you can buy hip-looking furniture at cut-rate prices, stylish pieces that often look like they came from more fashionable stores. You can have good taste here, or the illusion of it.

Which is to say there are also reasons not to like the big blue store. I could raise concerns about consumerism, about where all these materials are coming from and how their manufacture and distribution are wreaking havoc. There were also those horses found in its meatballs, the fecal matter in its chocolate cake. Its founder was once a Swedish Nazi, and even the company admits that in the 1980s some of its furniture was built by East German political prisoners. If none of this turns you or your stomach away, there's always the furniture itself to dissuade you, the designs that only look original if, like me, you don't know much about design.

Take IKEA's iconic Poäng chair, for instance, the cantilevered wood frame that curves like an S with the top cut off. It's a lovely chair, and quite comfortable, but it's a rip-off of a design by the Finnish architect Alvar Aalto, whose lounge chair 406 predates IKEA's by four decades. The differences lie in the quality of the materials and in the fact that you have to assemble IKEA's, which slightly undermines the fluidity you see in Aalto's design. And there's one other difference: you can still buy Aalto's chair, it just costs twenty times more.

One could argue that IKEA has brought the world of high design to the masses. We can all own a version of this paragon of style at a fraction of the price. Which brings me to the two Poäng chairs I bought one recent Saturday and assembled, beer in hand, in my living room. I had mixed feelings about buying them, and I hadn't even learned they were knock-offs yet, although I suspected something of the sort. In the showroom I was worried they might mark me, logically enough, as a *person who shops at IKEA*. I've never been fond of logos, but the more anonymous chairs I preferred were more expensive, and so my wife's will and my own cheapness prevailed.

If the episode means anything—if our decision to buy the chairs is at all representative of the decisions that take place at IKEA every day—it may be that the people who shop at IKEA are, above all else, on a budget. We are willing to privilege cost over integrity, but we prefer that style surrender little or nothing to cost. We are people with some measure of taste, but not nearly enough to see how and when we're being tasteless. We value pragmatism over originality. We are relentlessly bourgeois, and we know it.

That's one view of it. Another would note that Aalto's chair revises an earlier version designed for a tuberculosis sanatorium in 1933, and that this chair, named the Paimio after the sanatorium itself, borrows liberally from a metal chair designed by Bauhaus member Marcel Breuer a decade earlier. Breuer, in turn, claimed to have been inspired by his bicycle. In his mind, one imagines he bent the handlebars even more, stretching and shaping them into a chair. Aalto flattened Breuer's tubes into slats before refining further, and it was only years later when someone at IKEA figured out how to mass-produce what had initially been a bicycle and sell it for a song to people who might know the difference between a chair and a bicycle but not the difference between one iteration of an idea and the next.

2. Materials

The chair, simply put, is a marvel. What a delight it is to sit without supporting the weight of one's torso, to lean back and look out the window—at the squirrels, the blue jays, the light streaming in through the branches of an oak tree. To think that for millennia the chair was a symbol of power, often carved out of marble or ivory. The muckety-mucks in their palaces had chairs, but commoners sat on stools or benches, or else on the ground. It was only during the Renaissance that people began to realize how great the chair could be, how silly that so few could sit in one. The throne gave way to the armchair, the monarchy to the assembly, and the idea of a chair you couldn't sit in, a chair of limited utility, fell out of fashion. The meaning of the chair, withheld for so long, became meaning for people.

A few weeks after assembling my chairs, I visited the Barnes Foundation's new museum in downtown Philadelphia. I had been warned about the building, which paled, friends said, in comparison to the original, a peculiar mansion at the center of a twelve-acre arboretum, located in the wealthy suburb of Lower Merion. Built in the 1920s for the early pharmaceutical mogul Albert C. Barnes, the house was never meant to be lived in but to display Barnes's wide collection of late nineteenth- and early twentieth-century art, which is precisely what it did until, in 2002, the foundation he established to administer the collection announced plans—counter to the wishes set out in his will—to move to a new building downtown.

The new Barnes essentially replicates the old one. Even the layout on the walls reproduces Barnes's vision for the collection: the paintings are displayed as one would have seen them fifty years earlier, albeit in a new location. But for critics of the move, that little caveat makes all the difference. Jed Perl, writing in *The New Republic,* claims that "a replica of a room…has an effect on a visitor that is utterly if subtly different." "No replica of a space," Perl continues, "no matter how exact it may be, is anything but a poor substitute—a simulacrum." The original space, however, was no less of an imitation: its rooms were simulacra of rooms, and I can only imagine the experience of walking through the house was "utterly if subtly different" than walking through one designed for people, not paintings.

At least the new Barnes acknowledges that it is first and foremost a museum—one that does not merely simulate the spaces of the old one but preserves them. Whatever else the new building is, its primary exhibit is the old museum. It is a museum within a museum, a simulacrum within a simulacrum, and if walking through it is a degraded experience, it is nonetheless a strange and complex one. Imagine building an exact copy of the interior of the Guggenheim within a new superstructure. What would it be like to walk the new building's descending spiral? The copy could not help but point to the absent original, which a visitor would nonetheless inhabit through the copy.

Something similar happens at the Barnes. The architects have designed a structure that ensures you won't mistake the copy for the original even as it invites you to do precisely that. Approaching the building, you walk along a reflecting pond before taking a sharp left toward the entrance. The door is not in front of you at this point, but on your right. Once inside, you must turn immediately to the left to enter the small first lobby, then left again into a short corridor, before finally turning once more to the right, at which point you enter the much larger lobby that serves as entrance to the collection. This zigzagging is purposefully disorienting, and in entering the building you are not simply walking through a door, you are pushing your way through the various layers that exist between the outside world and the collection—layers that include the failed lawsuits to keep the Barnes at its old location. The framing structures (the reflecting pond, the small first lobby, the larger second one, the coffee bar, the gift shop, etc.) are precisely that: they contextualize our experience. They point at the thing but are not the thing itself.

But if the old building isn't merely being replicated in the new one, then what is? As much as I want to agree with those, like Perl, who prefer the original to the copy, the spaces that matter most in the collection, either now or then, are not the ones that surround the paintings but the ones that exist between them. Barnes arranged what he called his ensembles in terms of light and shape, but a chaste Renoir is also offset, on the opposite wall, by a salacious Courbet, a painting of a slaughtered pig by one of the crucified Christ. Barnes's arrangements force you to focus on the images and, more importantly, the relationships between them. Withholding the usual labels that identify artists and titles is another means to the same end: without the lure of the name, you must first accept the lure of the image. That this dynamic is not only intact but arguably enlivened in the copy is a testament to its success.

As for integrity, there may be no greater argument for replication than the one made by the collection itself. Art, Barnes believed, was a matter of theme and variation—a conversation about form that took place through the paintings, between artists and viewers, often over centuries and across cultures. Imagine concluding, on the basis of the *Mona Lisa,* that one should never paint a portrait of a woman again. It isn't precisely the same claim made by Barnes purists, but it amounts to, at root, a similar conservatism that insists some things cannot be improved upon and can only degrade as they depart from the original.

3. The Experiment

The idea is to construct a chair using only the materials immediately available to you, those items you might find in your office or the confines of your house. The only criteria for success is whether the chair "works," less in actuality than in theory: it doesn't matter whether you can sit in the chair but whether someone could theoretically sit in it, regardless of how well it's constructed and to whatever effect (e.g., the chair collapses). To the degree that we want to assess the chair in vacuo—to the degree that we want to view it objectively—a successful chair may be any set of materials brought together under the rubric of chair.

Elaine Scarry argues, in *On Beauty and Being Just,* that beautiful objects incite, even require, their replication. Scarry means more than influence here: she gives the example of Matisse "plagiarizing" the imprint of the palm tree for a series of paintings made in Nice. Matisse's paintings succeed, in her analysis, because of the originality of his plagiarism: he copies the beauty of the palm in ways it hasn't been copied before. Beauty here is something inherited or derived. It is a matter of copies.

But if we follow this line far enough it isn't long before we find ourselves in trouble, as, by Scarry's logic, the palm tree may also be a thief, having copied its beauty from some earlier, more fundamental form. If beauty is traceable through time, if there is an original beauty from which all others—copies of copies of copies—derive, beauty becomes static, even monolithic (whereas the vicissitudes of fashion, if nothing else, indicate otherwise: one era's fashion is rarely another's, even if trends are recycled). If beauty were solely, or even mostly, a matter of replication, it stands to reason that the new Barnes would not be a contested site. If, on the contrary, beauty is a conversation, then the objections to the building become part of its aesthetic (dis-)pleasure.

While it's tempting to conceive of beauty as a constant whose vestiges resound over time, beauty is also situational. It arises as conditions allow. It is difficult to imagine the experience of beauty inside a gulag, though some have certainly claimed to have found it there. But what's beautiful in the gutter, or the gulag, is rarely the same as what's beautiful on the terrace, and even supposing the two happen to align, they are often beautiful in different ways, for different reasons. The palm tree outside the homeless shelter may be as beautiful as the one outside the mansion across town, but how could the experience of the former possibly be of the same order as the latter, hemmed in as the shelter is by want, the mansion by plenty?

Few would say, I imagine, that either tree is only beautiful in that it both conforms to and departs from an ideal. So many other factors contribute to making a tree (or any object or experience) beautiful, factors that have nothing to do with the tree. Suppose in the end I don't find Matisse's paintings all that beautiful, much less the palm trees that inspired them. Suppose I find Joan Mitchell's abstractions to be more beautiful, Agnes Martin's even more so, and at least in part because *I don't like Matisse*. Suppose what moves me most in a work of art is not what it represents but, as Barnes believed, the way it invites me to look.

To see the original as no less conditional than the copy may just be more workable than the opposite, in which beauty is an ontological question. If any beauty I encounter is, by virtue of its being a copy, a mediated experience—and potentially degraded as a result—the world in which the work of art is created, or copied for that matter, becomes a secondary one on a hierarchy of being. My IKEA chair, like the new Barnes, is of a lesser order than the originals, themselves lesser versions of ideal chairs and museums. Were this the case—and I like to believe it's not, or at least not entirely—it could only be a disastrous situation for art. It would suck the air out of the space between the viewer and the view.

4. Hypothesis

It might not be enough to ask whether the chair works, whether it serves its purpose. Because in asking that question, I'm also asking another: does the chair work for a person in general and, more specifically, for me? Given that what makes for a good chair varies from one person to the next and from one discipline to another (e.g., furniture-making, architecture, history—even fields like criminology or religion, in which a stiff chair may be preferable to a cushy one), it's possible that the chair cannot be validated on its own terms.

Months before my fateful trip to IKEA, I watched Abbas Kiarostami's 2010 film *Certified Copy*, and, I now realize, something moved in me. I had already started writing this essay, which I wouldn't actually begin for some time.

The film is, in part, a copy of Richard Linklater's *Before Sunset* (2004), and like Linklater's film, Kiarostami's traces an itinerary from the relatively anonymous space of a public reading at the beginning to the intimate space of a bedroom at the end. The conversations between the two couples in each respective film are correspondingly progressive in their intimacy: *Before Sunset* presents two people falling in love (again), and *Certified Copy* slowly reveals that two apparent strangers may be a married couple.

Nothing much happens in either film. The couples walk and talk, and as they move through their rarefied European spaces—Paris and Tuscany, respectively—the camera doesn't leave them alone for a moment. It is as though we were watching the couples in real time, voyeurs to their private dramas. That we know little of what came before these snapshots, and nothing of what comes after, is an important feature of this particular brand of realism: the backstory is no more vital to the films than the resolutions to the conflicts within them. We have only the magnetism of the attraction (or repulsion) between characters to sustain us, and it is ultimately the muck of their relationships that entertains.

From there the films diverge, and the romance of Linklater's is, in Kiarostami's, replaced by a relationship that might not make it past the film's final frames. Kiarostami's film is also aware of itself as a piece of art in a way that Linklater's isn't. He relishes the metadiscourse around making; Linklater mostly avoids it. *Certified Copy* even takes a certain pride, per its title, in its status as a copy, and one of the claims the film makes is that a copy can be just as beautiful, if not more so, than the original.

Whether or not Kiarostami's characters actually believe that is another question. The husband in the film, James (played by William Shimell), has written a book about copies, and the argument for copies in and of themselves appears to be his. But in person he resists the copies of artworks they look at first in his wife's shop, then in a museum, and finally in a square the two visit. It appears to be the couple's anniversary (either that or their whole relationship has been condensed to a single afternoon), and they may be partly retracing the itinerary of their wedding day. But when they encounter a young couple on their own wedding day, James wants nothing to do with them, nor does he want anything to do with the most intimate of copies of and in his life—his adolescent son. For James, in short, delighting in the copy may be mostly an intellectual exercise, better in theory than in practice.

His unnamed wife (Juliette Binoche) is a more sympathetic character. She believes in the agency James's theory of copies gives the viewer: it means that what matters is the engagement a work invites. What is eternal in the sculpture they come across in the square—also a copy, we gather—is not its relationship to the original version but the gesture both original and copy enact: the woman placing her head on the man's shoulder.

James doesn't have time for eternity: he has a train to catch. Like Linklater's Jesse (Ethan Hawke), whose real name is James and whose flight home looms over the action in *Before Sunset*, Kiarostami's male lead is working against the clock. Where Jesse feels his departure coming too quickly, James's can't come soon enough. He appears increasingly bored and irritated as the film goes on, and the carefully constructed distances between him and his life collapse. He may be the proponent of the virtues of the copy, but the idea that his marriage might be an imitation—if not of other marriages than of (his) marriage itself—galls him. He has been trying to convince himself of his own idea. He has failed. The copy may be good enough for others, but it isn't good enough for him.

For James's wife, the question of the copy hardly matters in the end. She's more practical than that. She wants to live with the things that inhabit her life, regardless of how she might intellectualize them. You could almost say that insomuch as she's a mother mostly parenting their son on her own, she doesn't have a choice. The original is a luxury, a privilege she can't afford. She must abide the copies.

5. Results

On the surface, the experiment appears to have been a test of materials: if you have a lot of cinder blocks in your house, you will likely build a more durable chair than if you have lots of loose sheets of paper. But there is another dimension that has to do with the experiment itself: have you been testing the materials or have you been testing the idea of building a chair? Suppose it is this second layer of the experiment that intrigues you. Suppose you realize that rather than building a chair, you can substitute something for it—your heaviest dictionary for example. You call your dictionary a chair, and it is true that you can sit on it. You produce other such chairs out of wasp nests, chunks of graphite, vintage pornography, and fingernail clippings. Experts validate your chairs and produce their own out of flowers, legal testimony, and automobiles in turn. Eventually you are given an endowed professorship in chairmaking. You are invited on national TV. It's better not to know anything about making chairs, you say to the smiling host. Some chairs are not meant to be sat in, but both of you, naturally, are sitting in expensive ones.

If what's true of the unnamed wife in *Certified Copy* is true for viewers as well, is our experience necessarily diminished, our simulacra poor substitutes, especially if we don't know (or don't care) that the copy is a copy? Or, to turn that question around, whose experience is enriched by the originals if not those who possess them? The copy may glorify no one, but the original glorifies its owner most of all. What's strange is that, as viewers, we share the owner's concern. Imagine the person who would prefer seeing a copy of a painting over the original. Imagine the person who would willingly pay top dollar for a fake Matisse. And yet if you were to put the two side by side without saying which was which—if you could no longer rely on provenance—then it would be much harder, except in the case of greatly inferior copies, to develop a criteria of preference.

In the Barnes Foundation, for example, that copy of an art museum, I was drawn to a painting by Hieronymous Bosch. The visionary quality of Bosch's work has always stood out to me as something of a miracle: if ever there was an original, it was him. So imagine my surprise when, after a few minutes alone with the painting, an older couple entered the gallery and the woman told her companion, when they came around to the Bosch, that it was a copy.

I found myself unconsciously dismissing the painting as inferior, but was it? I had reacted strongly to the canvas before I knew it was a copy, but not because it was an original: the painting spoke to me on its own merits. Now that I knew it was a copy, would my appreciation dissolve altogether? Isn't this precisely the dilemma in which Kiarostami's James finds himself? Intellectually, he might argue that there's no reason why the copy in the Barnes should be any less admirable than the original, but he might nonetheless expect me to respond as I would to spoiled milk. Part of this kneejerk reaction could be no less evolutionary than my inborn sense to avoid foods that may poison me, and it could be that the copy, like the fake, is intellectually and emotionally dangerous, but *only if I know it's a copy*. If I don't, then my experience of it can be as authentic, at least in my own mind, as the viewer who has the means to travel to the Portuguese museum where the original is said to hang.

Then again, I may have it backwards. The copy may only be dangerous if I don't know it's a copy, since this could mean I'm being taken advantage of, as I might be should someone pass me a counterfeit twenty. When I know the painting is a copy, I still have the ability to enjoy it, even if I enjoy it as a copy, but I also would want to know—wouldn't I?—whether the twenty in my pocket is a fake. Unless the clerk in the gift shop doesn't know either, in which case I hand her the bill and the rate of inflation goes up an infinitesimal amount. Suppose a similar devaluation (of esteem, if nothing else) happens in the case of the Bosch painting—or in the art world as a whole—is that really as much of a problem for me as a viewer as it is for those who own the originals? Is the threat posed by the copy less of an intellectual than an economic one? Is originality in effect a currency, its defenders (and their elaborate defenses) akin to national banks?

6. *Analysis*

It is no doubt easier, and infinitely more practical, to sit in an actual chair rather than a conceptual one, but what's unsettling about the experiment is that, as everyone intuitively knows, no one spends $9 billion on a particle collider to study how it was constructed. That would be a bit like visiting Mount Rushmore to admire the blueprints. Either way, we have arguably returned to the Middle Ages, if we ever left them—producing objects of limited utility, objects of tremendous symbolic power (symbolic, that is, of power), whose meaning, for most, is prohibitive. Future readers in particular might peruse some of the strange language machines built over the past few decades (this one included) with no small bewilderment, as though they were deformed chairs, poorly designed, and which, ultimately, are not meant to be sat in. In lieu of an alternative program, or in advance of one, I can only record that the chair I have built out of discarded drafts of this report, though not altogether insubstantial, is insufficient to my frame.

If pragmatism trumps originality—if I am indeed someone who knows the difference between a chair and a bicycle but not the difference between one iteration of an idea and the next—then there should be no problem with the copy, regardless of whether or not I know it's a copy. But what Kiarostami's James feels in front of the sculpture—what *I* felt in front of my ersatz Bosch—suggests this isn't the case. It suggests that pragmatism only substitutes for originality when the latter is out of reach. And the problem of justice, which may reflect the problem of beauty after all, is precisely that the originals, or the conditions of originality, are so often out of reach.

There's something as bourgeois in cherishing the copy, then, as there is something elitist in cherishing the original, but whereas so few have recourse to such elitism, the conditions of most are manifestly those of the copy—or rather those of the copy of the copy, or the copy of the copy of the copy, as Baudrillard might say. Even our knockoffs are knockoffs. And as for beauty, you find it where you can. If its mediation isn't total, it may be near enough to obscure whatever remains of the genuine article, if that even exists. Of course, there's also something bourgeois in the semantics at play here, and I suspect that if I could only divorce my IKEA chairs from words like *original* and *copy*, I might finally answer the question I still haven't quite gotten around to asking.

Even then I would need a place to sit.

Much later that morning, as he moves southeast down Fairview, Subject remembers the opening of a video installation inspired by Friedrich Dürrenmatt's *The Assignment,* a book about surveillance told in long run-on sentences, one per chapter, sentences from which the reader can't escape, that's the point, and which had a glancing relationship to the network of cameras recording viewers as they passed through a series of rooms, their captured images cleverly remixed and projected throughout. The installation, Subject thought at the time, was like an elaborate hall of mirrors. The images might have been unflattering—in one he appeared to be picking his nose—but they were mostly, sometimes amusingly, mundane. The footage accumulated one megabyte after another, but the only narrative was the one that, as viewer and subject, he provided. Yet for days he considered walking through a second time as an inverse Hester Prynne, placard around his neck: *what if I have nothing to hide?*

This is in part his privilege speaking—he is a straight, white man in his thirties—the same privilege that allows him, at 10:41 a.m., while heading south on College Avenue, to stop at the corner of James Street and photograph the camera mounted to the streetlight, and then, a few minutes later, at 10:45, to repeat the procedure at the corner of College and Lemon, then again, at 10:47, at College and Walnut. Subject muses mostly on privacy at first, but as the morning proceeds he becomes interested in the illusion of it: how, in his short lifetime, privacy has degraded into a catchword. The city traffics in such illusions, none of which to his mind is more prominent, and more friable, than the appearance of order, that delicate balance between private desires and public concerns. A grid may impose this illusion on the chaos that accompanies and to some degree drives development—and the imposition may essentially take, most of the time—but what is surprising to him is that we should mourn the loss of something we never truly possessed, whether it's privacy or order or the uneasy relations, made plain in public, between them.

Figure 1: Socity.

Subject is sweating a little by the time he returns to view at 10:59, heading south at the corner of First and Crystal. He passes an overweight woman smoking a menthol and shouting obscenities at a neighbor on a nearby porch as the neighbor's young daughter, no more than five or six, clings to her mother's side. Subject pauses, confused both by the exchange and by the shifting angles of the streets, for while King and Queen run more or less according to the cardinal points, forming the x and y axes of the city, they break off at various angles, and in the asymmetrical gaps these divergences create whole neighborhoods have sprung up over the course of the city's history that obey their own internal sense of direction. He remembers well enough leaving the sprawling county park on Strawberry Street one afternoon and taking a right onto Chesapeake, not knowing that where it curves in response to the Conestoga River it becomes Broad, the street he was looking for. He reached Duke and, believing it to run north and south, turned onto it, not knowing that on this stretch it runs northwest and southeast. Because Subject was already confused, he turned right instead of left, heading, without realizing it yet, in precisely the wrong direction.

Two minutes later, Subject is at the intersection of Third and Crystal, at the southeast corner of Rodney Park. The place has recently been remodeled, and as he moves west along Third he notices the bundle of curved steel bars at the opposite corner. He passes through them wondering whether each of Lancaster's parks will be outfitted with these symbolic gateways, whether the city feels the need to underscore its spaces of exception, where the lives observed beyond their boundaries may be set aside, if only figuratively. What if the exception itself is the problem, he asks himself, or a manifestation of it, since we so often wear its necessity visibly—like a secret we're dying to tell—as outward distress.

Subject is now moving through a neighborhood called Cabbage Hill, so named for the German immigrants who settled there in the nineteenth century. The streets are densely packed with rowhouses and tiny treeless yards reminiscent of an English mill town. Shirtless children ride their bikes through potholed alleys. Old women walk to or from errands as

Figure 2: Threshold.

young men tinker with cars. Sunny patches alternate with shady ones, flat streets with sharp hills, industrious sorts with lumpens. Now and then the streets widen a little, or an empty lot opens out of nowhere. Suddenly Subject sees where he is in relation to, say, the Marriott that towers over downtown. Or else a long, descending street gives him a glimpse of the city as another place: San Francisco, he wants to say, but Baltimore is more accurate. Subject sees his share of posted notices warning of structures unfit for human habitation, and in some cases the justifications are visible from outside: porches falling apart at all angles, garbage strewn about the yards, grime and mold fogging the windows.

Some twenty-five minutes will pass before Subject reemerges into view, but he is spotted, at 11:11 a.m., by an officer entering his cruiser at the corner of St. Joseph and Fairview. Subject is doing nothing illegal, yet he feels, in this neighborhood in particular, observed by the officer, as though by the city itself. His posture stiffens, and as he quickly strides on he remembers hearing it said that the East German secret police, the

Figure 3: Condemnation.

Stasi, were effective because people policed themselves. They believed they were being watched, and that's all it took to rouse their self-censors. As much as he may want, in response to his own inner watcher, to raise the lid on the self, to bridge the internalized divide between public and private, he has a conflicted view of the self-exposure, possibly a form of indiscretion, that appears to be all the rage. The show *Girls*, for example:

there's empowerment in it, he can see that, but he is sometimes bothered that the characters have nothing to do but fuck, not so much each other as the men who fail, again and again, to understand them. Subject does not like the idea that we are just our genitals, walking sex machines whose brains function mostly as crutches to carnal ends. He doesn't like the idea because he suspects it's true.

Subject then remembers a young woman in matching pearls troubled by the vulgarity (her word) of a book he'd assigned. Did she mean the sex? Subject asked. Yes, she blushed, the sex. The perceived depravity, he said, is as much figurative as actual. In her descriptions is another laying bare, a separate state of undress, and when, as a writer, she submits her desire to our scrutiny, the power of its effect comes from the fact that she is wholly unabashed. Her fantasies are public, they are brash. And he admired that, he said. Some days later, the class was discussing a book by a second writer, a friend of his who also writes about her sex life but at a remove. Some of the encounters were regrettable, she admits, but instead of giving the details she flirts with readers a little, performing the textual version of leaning over to make visible the tiny bow in the middle of her bra, as she describes doing in the book. She's courting a man who will treat her like shit, not because of the way she courts him, but because of the man he is, selfish and incapable, also charming and cosmopolitan. The young woman who objected to the first book particularly liked the second, and though it might make him a hypocrite, given his opinion of *Girls*, something prudish, if unsurprising, stood out in her privileging of palatable desires over more explicit ones. She preferred the art of concealment, of modesty, of half-measures, even if such an art, in his opinion, holds too much back, is limited by its own decency, which has the effect of limiting readers as well.

We—but does it matter who we are?—pick him up again at the corner of New Dorwart and Fremont, heading northwest. It is now 11:27 a.m. and though not particularly hot the air is muggy, and Subject, wearing dark jeans and a t-shirt, is sweating considerably. He continues to contemplate Lena Dunham, the star of *Girls*, as though the question of self-exposure were a civic one. He admires her willingness to abase herself, which is also her desire that we should see ourselves, as viewers, abased. But Subject suspects this is the wrong word. Dunham has another edge to her. It isn't just exhibitionism, though there's that too: it's the wrinkles, hairs, and dimples that would otherwise be airbrushed out—in *Sex and the City*, say, which *Girls* both imitates and undermines. It's not exactly that he admires her willingness to humiliate herself, but rather how she embraces the suppressed body, how she embraces, even if it's a ploy, her humility. Because everywhere Subject turns there he is, or as Rilke wrote, "There is no place / that does not see you." And then: "you must change your life."

He wants to find something out, it seems, to learn whether in foregoing safety and disavowing all secrets all things become possible. To dis-close, he thinks, staring up at the sixth camera he's seen that morning, may be to enter the condition of being not-hidden, and if that requires unburdening oneself of one's secrets, so be it. To be human is to be embarrassed. Or so he tells himself, still safely cocooned in his privilege, as he crosses St. Joseph for the second time that morning, at 11:29 a.m. Four minutes later, when he crosses Manor Street and begins heading north on Old Dorwart, he remembers how, wanting to avoid the real or figurative pillory, he asked his class to write down a secret then to sit on it for an hour. In an alternate reality, he might have asked them to write their fantasies, sexual or otherwise, but in this one he couldn't or didn't want to. He remembers the mere presence of the secrets made them sheepish. They spoke less,

Figure 4: No place.

more guardedly, and when the time came to write about their secrets, near the end of the class, many covered their pages with their hands. He asked for volunteers to read, and as there were none he thought for a second, having also completed the exercise, that if he were to read his piece aloud students might open up and read theirs. There was no way for him to do this, he realized. He was a coward, worried about reprimands from deans or even getting fired.

He remembers writing that day about the time at nine or ten when he was naked in his room and his brother stormed in, looking for something of his: how he slammed his door on his brother's hand, how his brother shouted, how their mother came quickly up the stairs. Subject could hear her whispering outside his door, *it's totally normal,* and it was, or might have been, but Subject understood *normal* was meant in a private way. What did he feel then, he wonders, if not embarrassed, embarrassed that he had a body, that he was curious about that body, but that to be a body was indelicate, uncivil, and even though Subject would like to say he outgrew this embarrassment, he suspects it merely changed forms, morphed into the posture he adopts when someone he doesn't know comes too close, seizing up then backing away, the same embarrassment he still sometimes feels in stepping up to a urinal, ashamed to stand there in plain view. But it is more than that, really, ashamed of having to urinate in the first place, ashamed of being a body, of *being seen* as a body.

Soon Subject finds himself in the crumbling downtown cemetery where one of Lancaster's native sons, Thaddeus Stevens—memorably played by Tommy Lee Jones in Steven Spielberg's *Lincoln*—is buried. Stevens was a type of Republican they don't make much anymore, a fiery opponent of slavery and discrimination and an outspoken advocate for free public education. In nearly every portrait the corners of his mouth appear as though etched downward at sharp angles. He does not look like someone you would want to tangle with, and by all accounts he was a fearsome opponent. That a period follows his name is probably a graphological quirk of the time, but it also reflects the man's mouth. End of discussion, it says. Or, perhaps: *you must change your life.*

This is the scene in the film, Subject thinks in front of Stevens's grave, where he stands at an abyss, taking in the physical scale of the steep rock faces, the depth of the chasm. The music is both triumphant and

Figure 5: Graphology as metaphor.

melancholy, one quality even deriving from the other, though standing there in the cemetery he can't quite parse out which is which. But no, he's not in the scene at all, or rather so briefly that he might as well not be. What remains is the view of his absence, and what story, public or private, does it tell? The hours upon hours of empty frames, the watchers secluded in their (that is, in *our*) cubicles: we are mirrors awaiting reflections, he thinks, narratives awaiting expression.

It is August 22, 2014, a Friday under mostly cloudy skies, and exiting the grounds on Chestnut, Subject's walk takes the shape in his mind, as seen from above, of an upside-down question mark. It does not surprise him in the least, this sudden vision, and yet how acutely he feels it then, like an insoluble equation: the desire to be seen, the need to run and hide.

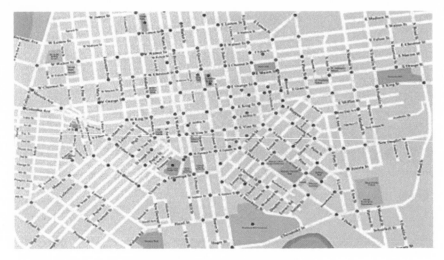

Figure 6: Open-air prison.

THE BLANKNESS OF BLANKNESS

The first paragraph of this essay is imaginary. It does not exist. What I'm writing here is not a placeholder for it, and should its absence not completely gall you, it may be necessary to construct it for yourself, what it might or should have said. It will be work, and for that I apologize at the outset, but omitting the first paragraph—as opposed to substituting this one for it—is more than a meaningless obfuscation or cheap gimmick. Such lacunae are the subject of this writing, the central difficulty around which I will circle, as though it were a lake in deepest summer. Let us begin there, at the dark pool—dip our toes into its murk.

Or rather here, on the opening page of Michael Ondaatje's *The Collected Works of Billy the Kid*, which consists of an unfilled frame, a black outline where a photo of the outlaw should be. Capturing motion, the photographer brags just below, is no longer any trick, and presumably the photo of Billy is one such shot. The discrepancy between the boasting and the blankness speaks volumes. Everything the book is, or might become, rests within that empty outline—and in the gap between what one imagines one is doing (capturing motion) and what one is actually doing (producing blankness). Everything the legendary outlaw was, or was rumored to be—everything he might yet become—awaits penciling in by reader or writer, but the picture's blankness defies such completion. The rest of the book, from actual photographs and dime-store novels to fractured sonnets and hallucinatory scenes imagined by the author, attempts to triangulate its subject within the space of its opening frame. It is pure possibility that is equally impossible, an impassable doorway, a portal without passage. Ondaatje's book doesn't end at the difficulty of accurately rendering a myth; it begins there. The difficulty isn't resolved; it becomes, instead, an emblem.

At the same time that I am eager to excavate Ondaatje's singular gesture, I am conscious of a part of me predisposed to impasse, as though within the frame meant for Billy I see myself as well. The problem of this writing, which it only makes sense to foreground, has less to do with literary history (except metaphorically) than with the certainty that Ondaatje's task—his vision of blankness—is also this and any reader's.

Begin again.

I write this in an emptying room. My keystrokes echo through the unfilled space, their clicks undampened by the previous contents. What is the space now that it wasn't just a few days before? What will it become without my last remaining things—a desk, a chair, a few pinned postcards—to give it texture? I am moving out of (and into) a house that has emptied dozens of times since its construction in 1924. The space is no less itself for my departure than for the absence of any other resident from the past ninety years.

Still, emptiness alters it for me, its present (though not for long) inhabitant. Once it invited me to fill it, but the license the room granted was limited, provisional. And the particular permissions I enjoyed here—white rug, brown bookshelves—say more about me than it. The dimensions remain sixteen by twenty-four. The relatively low ceiling (around eight feet) slopes along the east (back) and west (front) sides of the house, where it meets the walls at about six feet high. My desk sits in a small recess at the front, four or five feet deep and just as wide. A longer desk would not have fit up the stairway, let alone in the alcove. The walls could not accommodate taller shelves.

A room is a boundedness, an enclosure, an outline. It is a pregnant gap. It shapes more than takes shape. A room becomes what you want it to be, but only within bounds that are less reasonable than architectural. The woman moving into this house in a few weeks will approach the room as a (nearly) blank slate, configuring its vacancy according to her needs, as I have configured it to mine. I've used this space as an office, but I see no reason why it might not become a nursery, having raised one or two ideas here, except that the new resident, who must be nearing sixty, told me she probably won't use the attic much. She likes to be near her instrument, a grand piano she plans to install downstairs.

I am at a loss to say why I am sad to leave this particular set of spatial limits, although it channeled my work in a particular way. This is not the first space I've had to myself, but it's one where I've known some clarity and some light, of which the writing I've done (am doing) here may be a measure.

And again.

The true subject resists. It reduces where it wants to exceed. Which is to say: this was once a vastly different essay in a mostly similar room. Since then a space has opened between me and its ostensible subject, or do I mean its ostensible mode? I am meant to be—have set myself the task of—writing about *Spring and All*, the landmark 1923 work by William Carlos Williams. I find that, landmark or not, I cannot write about *Spring and All*. The essay I set out to write has transformed into a blankness dense enough to repel me. I do not know how to proceed.

I had meant to explore how Williams "prefigures many of the concerns of today's hybrid practice: polyphonic authorship, distrust of established forms, and a sense that the work 'teaches' the reader how to read it." I planned to argue that the book "derives much of its purpose from the impossibility of precisely articulating that purpose." I wanted to celebrate its interruptive moments, those times "when Williams suddenly suspends and defers the prose text in favor of poetry," and I wanted to claim that this kind of interruption is not only "central to his working method" but to "textual hybridity more generally."

Later, I revised my intentions:

> My goal is not to codify any sense of lineage or inheritance, but to limn the contours of the hybrid gesture then and now as a suspension of the act of writing that simultaneously situates the subject, and the reader, inside of that suspension. This is a nearly anarchic space, full of possibility, and I will argue that it is also, for writers, a site of tremendous permission. There is an urgency that arises when the sentence breaks into the poem, when a writer lets us hang in the space between one thing and another, and it is this urgency that allows or exhorts us to continually hybridize, isolating certain strains and joining them to our own.

I admire these sentences, written as they were by a self I do not recognize, whose capabilities are not my capabilities, or whose interests have changed shape in the intervening years. There is no path forward for me to reach them, or else I see no path leading away from them. There is only the gap between where I am now (an emptying room) and where I was then (a filled one).

I step away from the desk. First I am pacing in the attic, then I am running down the block, along the river, slowly working out why the subject feels foreign. It isn't that I don't like Williams, or *Spring and All*, or any of the other writers I had planned to connect to him: Anne Carson, Christian Hawkey, Bhanu Kapil, Michael Ondaatje, and Claudia Rankine.

I like them fine. Even, in some cases, a lot. But if you're reading this, you're smart enough to connect the dots between these writers and Williams. Probably you're smarter than me. You might write the essay I once planned to.

The Last Beginning

The gist of what I might have said ("Resist gist," advises Lia Purpura) is this. At the start of his landmark 1923 book *Spring and All*, Williams writes of the gulf that opens up between the reader and the world. "The reader knows himself," Williams says, "as he was twenty years ago and he has also in mind a vision of what he would be, some day. Oh, some day! But the thing he never knows and never dares to know is what he is at the exact moment that he is. And this moment," Williams continues, "is the only thing in which I am at all interested."

If instantaneity is what he's after, I might have written, he has a funny way of pursuing it. The form of *Spring and All*, as C.D. Wright says in her preface to the most recent edition, "spoofs the typographical stunts of the times, using both Arabic and Roman 'chapters' to fence off units of poetry and prose, completely out of sequence. *Chapter XII* appears upside down." The effect, she says, "creates a minor distraction, albeit intentional, but it is the abrupt shifting, cutting, and swerving that prevent the reader from ever relaxing into the text." Interruption is Williams's mechanism of immediacy, I might have gone on to say, one borrowed or adapted from cubist painters. The thing the reader never knows and never dares to know is here, where Williams' sentence

> ...the attempt is being made to separate things of the imagination
> from life, and obviously, by using the forms common to experience
> so as not to frighten the onlooker away but to invite him,

is interrupted by the poem beginning

> The rose is obsolete
> but each petal ends in
> an edge, the double facet
> cementing the grooved
> columns of air—The edge
> cuts without cutting
> meets—nothing—renews
> itself in metal or porcelain—

only to complete the sentence ("…things with which he is familiar, simple things—at the same time to detach them from ordinary experience to the imagination.") after yet another poem intervenes. Here the spring that has sprung is a distinctly modern one: *metal* has replaced *petal* by the end of the interrupting stanza, and a few lines later "copper [and] steel roses"—in the forms of skyscrapers, sculptures, or automobiles—appear. What Williams understands so clearly in these moments of splicing and severing is that the poem as rose—the poem as romanticized object—is insufficient. It requires sharper edges to achieve the reality Williams seeks.

I might then have interpolated several paragraphs about the *poete maudit* who "inhaled cholorform, drank absinthe, smoked cigarettes dipped in opium, read Rimbaud and Baudelaire and Poe and Verlaine, wore dandified clothing," and, allegedly, slept with his sister: Georg Trakl. I might have said that the writer Christian Hawkey's response to this cartoonish figure, in his homage to the poet, *Ventrakl*, is to approach the man from various angles: fake interviews, translations and mistranslations, biographical sketches, dictionary definitions, photographs, and Hawkey's own journals and poems.

I would have then pointed to the places in Hawkey's text, as in *The Collected Works of Billy the Kid*, where the impossibility of knowing one's subject manifests itself in the writing, when one plane of reality is perforated by another (à la *Spring and All*) and some third, hybridized reality takes place. Consider the following passage, which begins straightforwardly enough:

> George Trakl, born in Salzburg, Austria, on February 3, 1887, the fourth of six children, was regarded as the leading poet of German Expressionism. He was rumored to have intimate relations with his own *already you bore me*, although it's more likely that *I saw myself through deserted rooms.*

The passage—and others like it throughout the book—continues to swerve away from itself in the same fashion, as the authoritative voice of the literary biographer is interrupted by some chthonic shade of Trakl. I would have spoken of this swerve as a poethical wager, in keeping with the outline Joan Retallack provides in her book of that title. But while there is something ethical to the readerly interactions these texts invite, it may be an ethics necessitated not by any allegiance to form but by the subjects themselves. Impossible form here reflects impossible content, and the question of how to write compellingly about a rose might be the same as asking how to write ethically about it.

But this isn't that essay—or is it?

A Line Without Breadth, Part 1

Just now I was remembering a short trip I took to San Francisco in 2008. My memory of it arose while drafting an unrelated essay in which

I consider notions of boundlessness and drift, mostly as they pertain to jellyfish. But even as I say *unrelated*, the problem of the present essay emerges once again—the gap between one thing and the next, or the border the negation (*un-*) erects between them. As I try to reconstruct the trip, almost six years after it took place, I recall an exhibition focused on participatory art, or is it that—having looked it up on the internet—I want to remember standing in front of Hans Haacke's *News*, a teletype printer on a folding card table with a billowing heap of yesterday's dispatches piled up behind it?

Today I cannot draw the exhibition to mind, although I'm nearly certain, knowing my penchant for foregrounding the viewer (qua viewer), I would have seen it. The only thing that might have precluded a visit would have been the brevity of the trip, which couldn't have lasted more than 24 hours—I had a newborn to get home to. Whether I actually saw it in person or not—and as I write this I'm increasingly convinced that I didn't—the images of Haacke's piece, first realized in 1968, speak to something eternal in the writer's task, regardless of the automated composition of Haacke's text.

One word follows another as one second gives way to the next. But whereas one sentence compounds upon the previous one, the minutes drain away. It appears to be an inverse relationship in which one spends hours to accumulate pages. In writing one binds time, and the pages present, as much as ideas, an almost stratigraphical record. In reading one might sift through it, seeking signs of the gone author, or era. It is an inexact study, as words are inexact but inexhaustible, like time. One writes, one reads, but even if the material feeds in an orderly fashion, it may come out a mess at the other end.

More input is always arriving, as though from outside. A person can select the inputs that matter, however mattering is conceived, and run with them, or one can argue the inputs only matter in the abstract, which is what Haacke's piece (and much conceptual work) does. The particular news items are irrelevant, because when everything is news, nothing is. The facts multiply, but in *News* the proliferation alone stands out. Every day a tremendous amount happens, but if you look at the totality of events, nothing does, beyond the passage or collection of time.

In an art gallery, one might lose all track of it. One might forget the world outside of refined surfaces and rarefied spaces. One might forget, in '68 or 2008, places like Vietnam or Iraq, as I might forget, typing these words in 2014, the surge of unaccompanied children, mostly from Central America, across the US-Mexico border. Haacke's teletype speaks to that inattention: it punctures a hole in the exhibition. It isn't a memory machine, but one that brings the world to mind. It represents nothing so much as the insulated gap between what happens within and what happens without. The geology of the written word, time bound into paragraphs and pages, represents something similar, since any text is equally a matter of what happens outside of it. How the ruptures eddy and flow, how they undulate and inundate, and how a person can be both the vehicle for and witness to their motion.

Parable

Now we've come to a river. Not a particularly deep or dangerous one, but the water is cold, nearly freezing. We stare out, dumbstruck by the water's breadth, its indifference. We walk up the bank, looking for the best place to cross, and we have the good fortune to find some rocks in the riverbed to use as stepping-stones. What luck, really, but also what associative skill, linking one inertness, like one bank, to another.

I type one l-e-t-t-e-r after the n-e-x-t. The letters, once joined, form words. The words, sentences. The sentences, paragraphs. The paragraphs, pages. But it is as much discontinuity as continuity that defines these stepping-stones. The word is a word only because of the proximity of its letters to each other as well as their collective distance from the next bundle. It's the gap between that makes words what they are. Otherwiseyouhaveasentencelikethis. As a reader, you know this as much as I do, as a writer. It's a part of our contract so basic it does not bear mentioning.

Except that it does. It matters that a word is a little streak of ink between two white abysses. What comes before and after matters as much as what comes between. In this way a word is the opposite of a room, whose walls outline and enclose. A word is a room in reverse: a dense suspension of units (which have, in themselves, no part) that does not contain but excludes. A word, like the letters that comprise it, is what it is because of what it is not.

The implications fan out. Any text is only as good as the white spaces it contains. Or produces: the space between the reader and the page will not collapse, but it may be more or less charged by what lies on either side of it. And then those persistent ethical questions arise: how to mind the gap—in reading and in life. How to ensure against collapsing or expanding distances, or against confusing one (menacing river) with another (babbling brook).

To return, then, to our parable: one might have found other ways to ford the river. One might have built a dam, like a beaver, or the Army Corps of Engineers. One might have risked frostbite or even hypothermia. Or one might have said *fuck it,* and gone back the way one came.

A Line Without Breadth, Part 2

Maybe I saw that exhibition, maybe I didn't. I could be confusing a show I didn't attend with one or two others I did. I know for certain that three years earlier, in 2005, I attended a retrospective of Richard Tuttle's work in the same San Francisco museum where I might or might not have seen Hans Haacke's *News* in 2008. Tuttle's minimalism made an impression on me, which is ironic in that at the time I thought of his work, or parts of it, as *disposable*, for lack of a better word. I suppose even a minimalist can be wasteful, but I meant something like *ephemeral*, an art that touched lightly and left little trace. I meant the opposite of *monumental*, an art unlike the sculptor Richard Serra's (whose huge slabs of weathering steel I had walked through in Seattle) in scale if not in spirit.

What I really meant was *unassuming*. My favorite pieces in the retrospective were more than modest: they were humble. And I was struck by the contrast between the plainness of some of Tuttle's works and the relatively exclusive confines in which they were displayed. In one room Tuttle had pinned to the walls large swathes of colored cloth cut in polygonesque shapes. The point didn't reside in the fabric, exactly, but in the interactions between its edges and the walls. Tuttle had stripped the display of an artwork down to some bare essentials: an object, a wall, and something to hang the former on the latter. Beyond that, he had included shape and shade, but barely.

Another series of works consisted of wires mounted to walls but not flush against them, or not always, so that the overhead lights helped to cast thin shadows. Tuttle had also drawn curving lines in pencil on the wall, producing in effect three types of line: the wire itself, its shadow, and the pencil marks. I remember being astonished—a wonderful thing, astonishment—at how Tuttle had created so much from so little. I loved the interaction of simple elements intertwining and unfolding in multiple dimensions. I loved that such simplicity could house such complexity. And as art is a matter of line and light and shadow, I saw in Tuttle's work that, to paraphrase Daniel Tammet, a word, like a line, is a length without breadth.

The Borderline

In his late work on aporia, Derrida outlines three primary types of disjunction. The first "nonpassage," he says, "resembles an impermeability; it would stem from the opaque existence of an uncrossable border: a door that does not open or that only opens according to an unlocatable condition, according to the inaccessible secret of some shibboleth." Such aporias are as common as they are brittle: one need only erect a wall for it to begin to crack. They function through exclusion, and their categorizing logic is beyond familiar—sometimes productively, mostly not. On first glance, this seems to be the limit Williams confronts in *Spring and All:* the border between sentence and line that cannot be crossed. But while the white space between paragraph and poem might appear uncrossable—and while the meaning of one may not explicitly *carry over* to the other—the reader makes the passage nonetheless, much as she makes the passage between one discrete word and the next. The door does not open and still we pass through it.

Derrida's second type of impasse "stems from the fact that there is no limit. There is not yet or there is no longer a border to cross, no opposition between two sides: the limit is too porous, permeable, and indeterminate." Formally speaking, Williams's disjunction, like Hawkey's, appears to be of the first type—a line drawn across, or with, the text—rather than the second, but the border is in practice indefensible. Williams expends considerable energy in *Spring and All* dividing prose from poetry ("poetry does not tamper with the world but moves it"; "poetry feeds the imagination and prose the emotions, poetry liberates the words from their emotional implications, prose confirms them in it," etc.), but like the differences he outlines between reality and imagination, the text itself undermines, rather than reinforces, these divisions. Even as Williams insists on the sturdiness of the boundary between poetry and prose, his writing is a testament to its permeability, and the central impasse in *Spring and All* may actually be the indeterminacy of the borders it attempts to define.

"Finally, the third type of aporia," Derrida writes, "the impossible, the antinomy, or the contradiction, is a nonpassage because its elementary milieu does not allow for something that could be called passage, step, walk, gait, displacement, or replacement, a kinesis in general. There is no more path." Here, Derrida deigns to give an example: the syntagm "my death," which both signifies and grammatically enacts this aporia (i.e., *death* is the point beyond which *my* is no longer possible). It is also the aporia with which Ondaatje begins *The Collected Works of Billy the Kid:* a blankness that cannot be filled *except with its blankness*, even as it invites us to fill it.

First there is a path but it is blocked. Then the path becomes indiscernible from what surrounds it. Finally, the path and the surroundings themselves disappear. The impasses are distinct, but what unifies them is the way in which, Derrida writes, "passage and nonpassage are...coupled in an aporetic fashion," and in the way the negative form of the impasse (*no* entry, *no* limit, *no* path) is also an affirmation of the terms of the impasse. A border asserts that *this* is not *that* country, and in so doing reinforces the separability of *this* and *that*. (To delineate a borderline between poetry and prose is likewise to affirm a separability the hybrid disavows). One soon comes to see only the partition, and when waves of young children, for example, pass through it illicitly *one no longer sees the children*, only the terms they have crossed.

But it is the necessity of crossing, and its impossibility, that interests me.

The Third Type of Aporia

"The circle that pi describes," Tammet says, "is perfect, belonging exclusively to the realm of the imagination," and no subject (rooms, Williams, rivers) is any less perfect, which is to say indescribable. We keep at it, calculating pi to new decimals, but we are no closer to reaching the end of the chain than we are to cataloguing states of being. We live in a world we cannot describe. We keep describing it.

"Properly understood," Tammet writes, "the study of mathematics has no end: the things each of us does not know about it are infinite." The problem is hardly restricted to mathematics, and in the same week I read Tammet's *Thinking in Numbers*, I encounter the following, in an essay by Sven Birkerts: "No matter what one's subject, it is—in theory—inexhaustible." "Given world enough, and time," he continues, "all things can be seen to connect."

Divide any circle's circumference by its diameter and you arrive at the same number, pi. "It is an essential response," Tammet writes, "to the question, 'What is a circle?'" But he goes on to say that "this response—when expressed in digits—is infinite: the number has no last digit, no antepenultimate digit, no third-from-last digit, and so on. One could never write down all its digits, even on a piece of paper as big as the Milky Way." A circle may be finite and discrete, but its limitedness suggests limitlessness. Its roundness is at once familiar—one of a few basic shapes we learn to identify as toddlers—and incomprehensible.

I pick up a blue pen and draw a small circle on a piece of scratch paper. The figure before me is smaller than a dime but also larger than the galaxy. I delight in that doubleness, and I take from it a certain faith in these accumulating words, which will never be numerous enough to delineate their subjects. I draw a circle I call *Spring and All*. I draw a circle I call aporia. I draw other circles too, with names like Ondaatje and Derrida. They are outlines only, tiny figures committed to the nearest page to hand. At times they overlap, as in a Venn diagram, or a linked chain.

We live in a world we cannot describe. We keep describing it. The river is named *antinomy*. There is no more path.

The Blankness of Blankness

What is the blankness of blankness? What is the nature of its impass-ability? What lurks in the gap between one word and the next, the unfillable space that is also constitutive, a disjunction whose purpose is joining together?

The blankness I have in mind, to adapt a phrase of Derrida's, exceeds its borders at exactly the place where it experiences blankness (aporia, break). The interstices increase in direct proportion to the accruals (words, spaces), and though measurable (like a circle, say) they cannot be contained.

I wrote earlier of an essay I cannot write, a blankness that refused to be filled. And here I am filling it, albeit with other words than I had originally intended. I bow to the subject(s) I can only suggest. Thus the situation in which no progress is possible transforms, over weeks or months, into motion, so that I begin to wonder whether aporia can also become agency, or rather can allow for new forms of agency, whether the impassable sometimes becomes the threshing ground for the possible. If so, it matters. To the irreconcilable places we may find ourselves in reading and, more pressingly, our lives—it matters.

FLUTTER POINT

FLUTTER POINT (AN ESSAY IN THREE ACTS)

If you were to look for a person whose biography most reflected the twentieth century, you could do worse than Fritz Haber. The chemist who discovered how to fix nitrogen from the air, thereby creating the artificial fertilizers that enabled a dramatic spike in population, was the same innovator who adapted his process to make gunpowder, thereby fueling the massive death tolls of the century. The humanitarian who won the Nobel Prize for his discovery was the war criminal who pioneered the use of chemical weapons in the Battle of Ypres. The forward thinker who married the first woman to receive her PhD in chemistry from the University of Breslau was the repellent opportunist whose son led him one night in May of 1915 into the garden of his villa, where, after a party, his wife had shot herself with his revolver rather than remain married to him. Finally, the nationalist who renounced his Jewishness in favor of his Germanness early in his career was the exile who, persecuted by the Nazis, died en route to Palestine in 1934.

It would seem an instructive biography, but instructive of what? It's tempting to see Haber's life in terms of its painful ironies, to claim something like the law of unintended consequences at work, but it isn't precisely true that the outcomes ran counter to his intentions. Take the rise of a militaristic Germany: it was just such a nation, minus the anti-Semitism, that Haber, as a fierce patriot, had always aspired to and toward which his research was directed. Haber's remarkable successes were met, almost uniformly, by remarkable failures, if not of a professional sort then of a moral one. He was unable to meet the dilemmas of his time with any integrity, and it may be that along with his success came certain responsibilities that Haber refused, as he would any restraints to his personal trajectory. He appears not to have understood that his ambition was also one of those dilemmas, and that for his own good, if for nobody else's, it would have been best to accept certain curbs on it.

But then we may be more used by our genes than users of them. Life strives, and the primary purpose of living, at least on the genetic level, is to perpetuate life. The goal of the young chimpanzee climbing the social ladder is dominance, yes, but also the privilege to mate with the females in the group, thereby passing on his DNA. Human success may be less overtly sexual, but those ambitions have become sublimated in the drive for, among other things, professional conquest. Ambition may sometimes take hideous turns, but it is entirely natural to desire the best possible spot in whatever tribe to which you swear allegiance.

Because if the spot isn't yours, it's bound to be somebody else's, and that may not be something you can, in any sense, live with. Put another way, if Haber hadn't come up with the process for fixing nitrogen, it is almost certain someone else would have—not at the same moment, or even the same decade, but eventually. Science has a teleology to it, and once new paths are open they don't really close again, they just open further. This doesn't absolve Haber, but it does reframe the scope of his failings. If the age of synthetic fertilizers had simply come, and the age of synthetic gunpowder along with it, that might say as much (if not more) about the place we had arrived as a species as it does about Haber himself. And considering the heartlessness with which, on the whole, we have met the challenges of our age, I wonder if we weren't, throughout the twentieth century, a bit like the kitten who may know its claws are sharp but who hasn't quite learned to be careful with them.

For those of us equally unwilling to be either shrinking violets or total Machiavellians, it must be possible to proceed with some measure, however small, of compunction. If success sometimes amounts to good fortune, it must at other times be a product of the sense to balance one's ends with the costs of achieving them. And if this is the case for a single person, one would hope, given the dramatic prices we've already paid for our collective ambitions, it is equally true of the species.

Still, those Chinese alchemists scraping potassium nitrate from stone walls more than a millennium ago were only doing what made sense to them. They were exploring, experimenting, and their primitive methods were aimed at discovering something like the philosopher's stone. They may not have hit their mark, but they were aiming high, at something that didn't exist. Instead they found the saltpeter that came to be known as China Snow: the first gunpowder. What a delight it must have been for them to see the colors of the flames different combinations of the material produced. What a delight to their masters when they realized it could be turned into a weapon.

END OF ACT I

Imagine you're attending a performance, maybe in that big room at MoMA where Marina Abramovic spent several months simply sitting with whoever showed up. It's the night of the debut, and the gallery is packed in around what appears to be a small chamber, fifteen feet wide, covered in heavy drapes.

People mill about for some time. The waiting, you think, must be part of the performance, but some, they could be the smart ones, sneak out the back. You resist the urge to follow, and finally the curtains are raised, revealing two people, a man and a woman, in a sound-proofed glass box. They are yelling at each other, screaming really, but it's impossible to hear what they're saying. It is as though someone has hit the mute button for them, too, as neither appears to be aware of the audience.

After twenty minutes or so—more people have left in the meantime— the man reaches into his pocket and pulls out a pistol. He waves it around histrionically before pointing it at the woman, now hysterical, frantically clawing at the walls of the room but still unaware of the audience. You don't see the bullet, but in the brightly lit gallery you do see the small cloud of smoke, the pool spreading out from the woman's collapsed body.

There are gasps in the space. Screams. The curtain descends and the room explodes into anarchy as people pile out. The murder was real or it was simulated—there is no way to tell. You assume the latter, but then why did the museum ask you to sign that waiver?

Or suppose the performance takes place in the open. Suppose, as in Abramovic's, the only thing separating you from the artwork is a white line drawn on the floor. What are your responsibilities when the decision is not just a matter of endurance but one, potentially, of intervention? The role of viewer transforms into witness, and one's limited agency in the first scenario widens considerably in the second.

Here as elsewhere, responsibility increases in direct proportion to that agency. The more capable you are of action, the more culpable you become for what occurs. But again you don't really know what you're watching, or if you should even be watching it, nor can you claim any mastery over the outcomes. Maybe the woman will rise after the audience has rushed out, clean herself up, and get ready for tomorrow's performance. Maybe not.

From the hypothetical to the actual: Yoko Ono walks on stage at Carnegie Hall. The year is 1964. She carries a big pair of shiny scissors and the simple instruction to cut. The audience does as it's told. One young man turns toward the camera as he settles into his task. "It's very delicate," he says. "It might take some time."

She's been stoic up until this point, but now she bites her lower lip as he cuts off her slip. Her eyes dart back and forth. She's blinking a lot, nervously looking down at his work, her shredded dress. Someone calls out, "Make a piece for *Playboy*, Richard."

I watch the film on the second floor of the Hirshhorn. It is November of 2013, fifty years after the performance. My wife and son are in the neighboring Air & Space Museum, looking at moon rocks and rovers. He wants to know, she says in a text, when we're going to Mars.

Ono's *Cut Piece* is part of an exhibition on art's obsession, in the atomic age, with destruction. Although much of the work is highly critical, it's clear we are also (artists and viewers) partaking in a perverse entertainment.

People cycle through the gallery as I watch. I want to stop them, point to what radiates from the face of that zealous young man, linked as it is (in different ways) to both Abramovic and Haber, but some inkling of what I might see in their own, or they in mine, sends a shiver up my spine.

END OF ACT II

For a long time I was a poet. Then, suddenly, I wasn't a poet anymore. I'd like to say I traded poetry, as Sarah Manguso writes, for a longer life, but the truth is that one day poetry was there and the next it was not. I've had only one relapse, brief and intense though it was: in December of 2011, I wrote thirty or forty poems under the rubric "Flesh Forest" before I learned it was the name of a noisy garage band whose music, when I found it on the internet, I didn't really like or even understand. So I left the poems, and the music, alone, and when I turned to them again several weeks ago, wondering whether I might still be a poet, I immediately came down with a painful (and, for someone my age, rather rare) case of shingles.

But there are many ways to tell this story. On a hot August day, for instance, I took my son inside of a heart. It was made of narrow hallways and stairs, and the route was designed to mimic the passage of blood through its chambers. The heart—and the museum that surrounded it—was recompense, my way of making amends for the kittens I'd returned, after only a week, to the shelter.

That version of this story starts well enough, with friends celebrating the playful new additions. My eyes watered but that was the extent of it. The weather was lovely and the windows were open. We drank beer and talked and every once in a while someone would walk over to pick up and coo at one of the cats. A few days later, after they had pissed on the couch and rubbed their shit on the floor, I felt my throat constricting. It was warmer, more humid. We closed the windows and turned on the air. I woke up coughing, unable to breathe. We spent the whole day out of the house, and the following one as well.

The solutions (air filters, allergists) were costly, drawn-out, and for me, at least, unpleasant. The idea came over me all at once, out of nowhere, and with a force I didn't understand, couldn't reason with: I have to get rid of these kittens. Once it settled in my mind, like the cough in my lungs, I couldn't dislodge it. I was repulsed by the kittens, as though my body, for its own sake, were telling my emotions to stay away. I even felt contempt, which may make me the first person in history to have felt that way about a kitten.

Were she to write her own account, my wife might describe other such times in our life together when my reactions have defied explanation. I imagine her describing me as someone who makes emotional decisions, often irrational ones, someone who does or doesn't do something because it does or doesn't feel right, whatever that means. Someone highly, though suspiciously, attuned to his own distress. This may or may not align with her perception of me, though it does explain my response to the cats, to the poems, and even the genesis of this essay, its various acts that constitute something like a premonition.

We know more than we know, which is only to repeat a psychological truism: what happens in the mind and body, outside of conscious thought and action, has tremendous power.

Either my shingles meant nothing or the stress of the poems, like that of the cats, was simply more than my nerves could handle. Sitting in the shelter's parking lot last August, wiping the melodrama from my eyes, I thought that there must be something to perceiving these visible products of invisible processes, to knowing ourselves through our disturbances as they push their inexorable way, like the tips of various icebergs, to the surface.

END OF INTERMISSION

Four months after the opening of the Tacoma Narrows Bridge in July of 1940, a strong November wind blew in and the bridge began first to ripple then twist violently back and forth. In the 16mm footage shot by the owner of a local camera shop, the wavelike motion of the bridge is strangely captivating. A lone car is visible at its center and then, a moment later, a balding man with a mustache walks toward the camera. This is Bert Farquharson, an engineering professor, and he has been out to the car to try to save the cocker spaniel its owner, one Leonard Coatsworth, abandoned inside it. The dog, understandably terrified, has bitten him, and when the bridge eventually collapses that morning, Tubby the cocker spaniel will be the sole fatality. Coatsworth, an editor at the Tacoma newspaper, will say that "with real tragedy, disaster and blasted dreams all around," what appalled him most was having to tell his daughter her dog was dead.

In his 1958 film *A Movie*, Bruce Conner splices the failing bridge into footage of sinking ships, mounds of corpses, mushroom clouds, and even the crash of the Hindenburg. The images flicker on screen, interrupted by unexpected stretches of black leader, surprising intertitles, and the images Conner constantly juxtaposes against one another. The film moves forward excitedly, irregularly, and although it is clearly about "The End," as one early intertitle suggests, it equally enacts that ending, sputtering out as though history culminated in short, sharp bursts. Humans are so often fumbling their way through Conner's film, falling off or crashing into things, that the Hindenburg, like the atom bomb, appears to be the ironic pinnacle of human achievement, as though the progression of humanity in general, or technology in particular, could only ever be a march into deterioration, as though every bridge were always threatening to collapse.

The film manages to end, for all that, on an ambiguously optimistic note, with footage of a diver swimming through a wreck. Drums pound, cymbals crash, and the strings and horns hold one long, dramatic note as the camera turns up toward the lambent sun dancing on the surface of the sea. It feels like the end of a big budget picture from Hollywood's golden age, the top half of a double feature, but the play of Conner's title with the B-movie materials out of which his film is made hammers home the fact that we're never sure, in all this breaking up and falling to pieces, whether we're watching the main show or the warm-up act, whether the images foretell causes to come or merely recast old effects.

The collapse was caused by flutter, the technical term for the oscillation in the structure brought about by the wind but aggravated by the design, which caught the force instead of allowing it to pass through. Tacoma Narrows became a textbook example of how not to build a bridge, but the phenomenon also had other iterations. When, in September of 1959, Braniff Airways Flight 542 disintegrated mid-air near Buffalo, Texas, or when, six months later, Northwest Orient Airlines Flight 710 likewise disintegrated near Cannelton, Indiana, killing fifty-seven passengers and six crewmembers, the cause was ruled to be a form of flutter. Essentially, the wings and outer casings were too stiff, and once they began, due to a combination of speed and conditions, to vibrate unexpectedly, there was no way to dampen that motion. The wings passed it on to other parts of the aircraft in turn, which led even the fuselage to come apart at the seams.

These days all manner of structures are designed to accommodate the forces that can, if not properly accounted for, cause serious damage. Skyscrapers, for instance, are built in such a way that they sway slightly around their sturdy cores, and engineers have also designed gigantic dampers to counteract the effects of strong winds, including one filled with 300,000 gallons of water and another consisting of a 730-ton steel pendulum. Still, experts acknowledge there are stresses no building is designed to withstand, stresses that might, like that wobbling bridge, stem from an initial structural failure but lead to total collapse.

There are points in every system, even the psyche, when a disturbance becomes so acute that the whole thing starts to wobble and shake, when collapse first becomes possible and then inevitable. Beyond 350 parts per million (ppm) of carbon dioxide in the atmosphere, climate also becomes unstable: melting glaciers, extreme weather, rising sea levels. Since 1958, when measurement began under the supervision of Charles Keeling, these levels have been continuously monitored at the Mauna Loa Observatory in Hawaii, and the graph that now bears Keeling's name shows a steady upward curve. Some scientists say we have already reached a point of no return, others that we're fast approaching it. The analogue that comes to mind is an aircraft disintegrating mid-air, stressed beyond capacity by a turbulence it wasn't designed to withstand.

We see the signs and, in our various ways, we refuse them. I am as guilty of this as anyone.

Walking through Point Pleasant, New Jersey, the week after "Superstorm" Sandy blew through, I saw the debris piled in the streets, or else bulldozed into one of the enormous mounds in the parking lots near the beach. I stopped to look through a heap of old books between my brother's house and the shore, on top of which an old hardcover copy of *The Sound and the Fury,* now ruined, whiffled in the breeze like a warning—or a judge.

He blundered on in the cluttered obscurity, I remember reading. And, repeated just below it, *you bastard.* I stared at it intently, and at the moldy copy of *Treasure Island* right beside it. Nearby were sodden piles of the *New York Times* bound in twine, a paperback copy of the poems of Robert Browning, books on ethics, statistics, and American history, including one opened to a copy of the United States Constitution.

After a few minutes of this particular disaster (for how much could I take?), I turned again toward the shore, unsure of what I'd just seen, or what it meant. I knew there was venom in it, but it's taken me more than a year to feel the effects, which isn't the same as stopping the sting.

FINIS

FLUTTER POINT

I am trying once more this morning to write about blindness, having failed so many times in recent months that I must now admit I have no idea what it is to be blind. My own blindness, if it can be called that, is to the nature of blindness. I have to feel my way through my subject by touch. The dominant sense will not suffice, but then it rarely does, even for those of us who can see.

"Men are so blind that they even take pride in their blindness," Augustine writes, but he is speaking of blindness as a metaphor, much as, more than a millennium later, José Saramago imagines an epidemic of blindness, as pejorative in his hands as in Augustine's. The connotations are so recurrently negative, one wonders what a blind man would make of it. The only parallel that comes to mind is that of blackness, which in its figurative sense is so often associated with doom and gloom that one would be forgiven for accusing the lexicon itself of racism. As for the lingual prejudice against blindness, the suggestion is that discernment decreases in step with sight, but there is equally the counter-tradition whereby the blind—Homer, Milton, Borges—are endowed with insight, and even Saramago admits that only in a world of the blind might things become as they truly are, not as our attentions would make them.

The poet Mary Ruefle gets at the problem another way. She tells the story of a blind woman who briefly regains her eyesight after an operation: "the bite-sized leaves and red shreds" of the lettuce terrify her, but after five days she lapses back into blindness, having had her mental image of the world, or at least the lettuce within it, definitively shattered. Also surprising, Ruefle writes, is the fact that the blind woman often travels while Ruefle, or the speaker of the poem, rarely travels at all, even though in her dreams she often finds herself in Cuba, "walking among fronds with nothing to do / but watch red lizards climbing the wall." "Of course I have never been to Cuba," she writes, "but it remains a place / where I have never found it necessary / to alter my description of anything."

That the blind woman's experience does not correspond to her sight may be terrifying, but what is the shape of that terror? There is a certain shock to the real, and some artists might tell you it's their job to expose it. But the poem also presents a woman whose experience of Cuba in her sleep is rich and luxuriant, complete as is. For her, the world may be everything, but it also isn't everything. If it were, what use would there be for dreaming? What use would there be for art?

This question also haunts Wallace Stevens, who compares—in his own tropical poem, "The Idea of Order at Key West"—a song sung at a bar on the beach to the sound of the ocean. "She sang beyond the genius of the sea," he begins, setting apart at once the world and its art with that single word, *beyond*. Whereas the singer is "the single artificer of the world / In which she sang," "the dark voice of the sea," for Stevens, is "sound alone"—"meaningless plungings of water." There may be a world that is *merely* world, but the artist, like the dreamer, is not interested in what is not more than itself. Here, the idea of art stands in opposition to sheer existence, as by its nature art always moves beyond that state of *nothing other*. "It was more than that," Stevens says, "more even than her voice, and ours." While one effect of art, or of a dream for that matter, may be that it heightens the world as we live it—a song can make the sea or sky, even love or shame, more acute—imagination may also be more real than reality. For the singer in Stevens's poem, imagination *is* reality. "[T]here never was a world" for her "[e]xcept the one she sang and, singing, made."

Many months ago now, as I was beginning to ruminate on blindness, I heard a conversation between two blind men on the radio. The first, John Hull, refused to live what he called a life of nostalgia. If an image popped up in his mind, he would immediately extinguish it. Rather than picturing his wife's face, he would focus on her perfume, the texture of her hand, her embrace. This, he felt, was more honest than the alternative, a world of remembered images that no longer conformed to his sensory reality. Besides, his wife was aging, and any memory of her face wouldn't do justice, or so he reasoned, to the woman guiding him along the platform and up the few steps into the train.

Zoltan Torey, on the other hand, had never seen his wife's face and so was spared the pitfalls of remembering it. Unlike John Hull, such imagelessness wasn't a comfort for him, and he actively constructed her picture in his mind. He became convinced that this image matched her precisely, that by the power of his imagination alone he could create the visual world his condition had denied him. This was more than consolation, he believed: it was a workable model of the world. And when some tiles came loose on his roof, he set out to prove it, climbing up a ladder to fix them. His neighbors thought he was insane, but for Torey there was no reason to believe he couldn't act on what was true in his imagination.

It struck me as I listened that these two contradictory impulses—to attend to the world you've been given and to imagine a world you haven't—have almost everything to do not only with the singer in Stevens's poem but with why any of us make art in the first place. What precisely is it that a man like John Hull—who resists, by circumstance and choice, not only red and black but large and bright—attends to? Senses, impressions—the things out of which Zoltan Torey constructs his imaginary rooftops.

I am not interested in longing to live in a world in which I already live, writes Maggie Nelson, but which world is it one lives in, apart from longing? Does a person long for a world, or does she live in a world built from her longing, out of all she has lost?

When it became clear to Borges that he had "lost the beloved world of appearances" and would never fully regain his sight, he began a study of Anglo-Saxon, and the rich aural world of its poetry replaced the vivid colors all around him. Out of this new consciousness, he dictated poems line by line, and his blindness became an instrument that, as a writer, he harnessed. Blindness became a gift: that he might "make from the miserable circumstances of [his life] things that are eternal or aspire to be."

An artist may be a person who has lost the world, a person who, like Borges, in some sense, has become blind to it. I try, through my work, to create (or reconstruct) a world from the straitened circumstances of my life—narrowed both by my own limitations (there are always more than one would hope) and by my death, which is always right around the corner, even if it's years away. Art produces, almost as its primary function, an elaborate version of these losses even as it attenuates them. You hang up one measure of accuracy in favor of another, and it is, to borrow a description, as if the scene "occurs just above the surface of things, in a place where evidence becomes so light that it dissolves."

For the dentist in a Roberto Bolaño story, it's a mistake to say that art is one thing and life another. We convince ourselves that our lives are less significant, and so less deserving of attention than our art, but according to him we have it backwards: art, the dentist says, "is the story of a life in all its particularity...the expression and, at the same time, the fabric of the particular." What's more, he argues, there's something almost mystical about not just living one's life to the full but making art out of that intensity. This is "the secret story," he says, "the one we'll never know, although we're living it from day to day."

It's true that you cannot safely divide your body from your body of work, or that to do so may only be possible from a privileged position. The idea that you are not your work speaks to me of class distinctions, of those who have the leisure to identify themselves with something other than their labor. But one must also say it, head held as high as one's able: *guilty as charged.* Art may not be an exemption from life, but it is an exception to it, by its nature both a product of living and that which is extruded from a life. Art is moved matter, and though it may move one to any number of ends, though it may rouse the mind and quicken the heart, it is not animate.

Put another way, the world is either outside of us or else there is no outside. The internal world is either embedded in our biology, awaiting some diligent scientist to uncover it, or the internal world is all that there is, our most profound social and genetic inheritance.

For Stevens, when the song ends and he turns back toward the town, it appears that the outside has been colonized by the inside, or enchanted by it, and in ending the poem he returns to a sentiment he uncovered years earlier in writing of a jar placed on top of a hill, thereby creating the wilderness around it. For Stevens, there was no outside until we invented one, which could only mean that blindness is a condition that may not originate in the mind but is dependent upon it. If you didn't have a mind, you couldn't have a world, visual or not. Blindness may not be simply a physical or metaphorical condition, but an epistemic one.

Six months have passed since I began this essay in a car speeding north through Hartford. A big storm had blown through the day before, and snow was plowed up along the sides of the highway. The same chill that had regularly driven Stevens south, to the other pole of his existence, permeated the air. Since that time, I have added and removed many paragraphs, scraped away the remnants of various dead-ends I didn't at first recognize as such.

In my blindness, I begin again to finish what I've started, to assail my subject once more, which now takes the shape of a scene from Pedro Almodóvar's *Broken Embraces* in which the blind screenwriter, Harry Caine, stands over his assistant as he reconstructs a pile of torn pictures. The shot is painterly, with shreds of images covering the full surface of the coffee table, like a mosaic. The moment is charged with Harry's shattered identity: at the time the photos were taken he had gone by his given name, Mateo Blanco. He had been a director then, and the woman with him in the photos, Lena, was the star in his last film. She died in the same accident that robbed Mateo of his sight, transforming him into Harry Caine.

The practical dilemma is also the metaphorical one: the world is worse than a puzzle, it's a jumbled mess. And though we may succeed at reconstructing certain portions of it, the lines of fissure persist, as there is only so much we can see. For Harry, the predicament is magnified by the fact that he cannot examine the images on the table in front of him but is instead their walking embodiment. He is fissure in the form of a man: he writes for films he'll never see.

But there are so many films here. There's Mateo's last, which recreates Almodóvar's breakthrough, *Women on the Verge of a Nervous Breakdown*. There's the documentary about the making of Mateo's film, shot by the sinister son of Lena's jilted ex-lover, Ernesto. There are the films on Harry Caine's shelves: Fritz Lang, Jules Dassin, *Fanny & Alexander*, *Eight and a Half*. And there's Jeanne Moreau in *Elevator to the Gallows*, the film they're looking for when, near the end of *Broken Embraces*, Harry hears the soundtrack from his own film, *Girls and Suitcases*, on TV.

When he decides then and there to re-edit the whole thing, it matters immensely—both for Harry and for this essay—that he will do so in the dark, comparing the pitches of various takes. What he knows, he must intuit from his actors' voices. He will play his world by ear. But then the important thing is not to see the work but to see it to its completion. You have to finish a film, he tells his young friend, even if you finish it blindly.

Regarding the double I didn't dare to be.

In June of 2004, I moved to New York to be a writer but took menial jobs instead, answering phones at a firm in the Citibank building, for instance. The work involved spreadsheets and stock prices, catered meals and armed guards. I hardly wrote a word. So I took another job at a bistro on the Upper West Side, where before our shifts we sampled the wine list with a sommelier who looked a little like David Lynch. We ended the same way we began, with a drink, and on late nights, to my wife's consternation, I shared a taxi downtown with a pretty MFA student at Sarah Lawrence. As usual, Mexicans and Central Americans worked in the back and after long shifts took long subway rides to parts of Queens or the Bronx I had never heard of. I told them the few jokes I knew in Spanish, and while I supposed at the time this endeared me to them, I now suspect I played a different sort of white fool: the one who pretended to understand, as opposed to the one who couldn't care less. I had no more moved to the city to be a waiter than to answer phones, however, and the struggling actors I worked with at the restaurant set a negative example: I didn't want to spend years tricking myself into believing I was coming any closer to my goals. One day in November I called the manager to say I wouldn't be returning. I packed up the apartment that morning and skedaddled, tail tucked between my legs.

Because no place is without its lint.

It isn't so much that I want to dispense with time as with its effects, the shame and guilt and regret that any life churns up in its wake. Nor am I under any delusion about future disappointments, in myself or in others, but in looking closely at my orbit and the forces that compel it, I hope to dodge a few asteroids. I wonder less about what's pelting me with figurative rocks, blocking me from being the person I want to be instead of the person I am, than about whether that desire for improvement comes from the fact that the sentence moves forward in spite of itself, the paragraph even more so.

Of a self that isn't static in a body that isn't either.
Frank Mouris's 1973 short, "Frank Film," sums up his life in three simultaneous threads: a stop-motion animation of images that, Mouris says, appeal to him; a mundane, almost sentimental monologue about his progression from childhood to a career as a filmmaker; and played alongside that voice track, a second one consisting of associative lists relating to the first (foods, names, dates, etc.). Though only nine minutes long, it's still impossible to take it all in at once: you have to choose which thread to follow. The most obvious is the linear narrative, which, while no truer than the other two, may be what our brains are most programmed to process. Given the alternatives, we take the easy route, the familiar story, the version that proceeds from past to present. But Mouris's film insists this is only one of many versions of a life, that it is equally a stream of images—an animation of them, even—and a heap of language. We can, and probably must, develop an architecture to order all this data, but the real question for Mouris—and, I suppose, for all would-be autobiographers— is how do you prove, through the imposition of an arbitrary structure, that your life has been worth living?

Those things one consigns to oblivion.
I should add, before I go any further, that today is my thirty-fourth

birthday and that earlier this morning I scanned a number of websites with titles like "Twenty-five things to do on your birthday." There were many suggestions, including writing a letter to your future self, photographing everyone you love, and taking an extra-long walk with your dog. It was proposed that some of these activities, if repeated, could even become traditions, and that over time one might use them to tell the story of one's life. The idea I found myself most drawn to, at least in theory, came from the person who, on his birthday, bought a cheap box of dinnerware at a thrift store then smashed it all at an old factory. This year my birthday falls on a Sunday and the Salvation Army is, regrettably, closed. I do not own a dog.

Even dear things come apart, tattered books slowly unstitching themselves.

For six months I carried around an essay on structure by the writer John McPhee. I printed it out in January but didn't read it until July. I'm not sure why I was slow to come around, but it may have to do with my resistance to the organization McPhee is so good at. I've never been one to plan my approach, though I have sometimes wished I were. I proceed by trial and error instead, in fits and starts. I feel my way forward—always have. The dilemma of structure, McPhee writes, often stems from the "considerable tension between chronology and theme." Chronology usually wins, he says, for predictable reasons. We're used to linearity, to experiencing time as a progression through fixed points, and this is nowhere truer than in our accounts, the narratives we spin out of our lives or imaginations. But sometimes the chronology is pointless, McPhee adds. Sometimes the progression is not forward from A to B to C, but back and forth, endlessly, between A and B, or circular, or erratic. Times when time itself is incoherent.

In retrospect one always feels differently.

Those months in New York left a bad taste in my mouth. I was bitterly depressed and for the first time understood that drinking makes matters worse, though I still couldn't see the real shape of my struggle. I hadn't yet learned that depression comes in waves, which is what I said recently to the friend sitting across from me at the bistro, nine years after I last walked out its door. We had been to see the Bill Brandt exhibit that afternoon at MoMA, and afterwards, while walking in the park, it occurred to me that we might as well stroll over to the restaurant for a drink. I had a couple of hours to kill before my train, and though the idea of walking into the place first filled me with a twinge of dread, once the idea was planted I couldn't uproot it. Inside, nothing had changed. The same red banquettes, the same wicker barstools, the same sommelier slightly drunk in the back. I recognized one of the waiters, but did he recognize me, I wondered—did Patrick, the sommelier? By the time a second round arrived, I didn't care. I was replacing a negative memory with a positive one, and when eventually we stood up to leave I wondered whether, nearly a decade later, it was possible to do the same with the whole city.

Is there any moment that is not other moments besides?

It is November of 2004. It is March of 2013. It is June of one year, August of another. I am twenty-four or thirty-three years old. Six months have passed since I moved here. Nine years have gone by since I left. I have no real ideas about time, no sense of what it means for life to recur. Or I suspect that I am already living my life over—that time consists, in part, of bridges that turn back on themselves. While a life would appear to be a matter of chronology, my own experience is at once order and circularity, inconsistency, contradiction, and in recounting my life, or the experiences it comprises, there is simultaneously no structure that would be more sensible and more pointless.

Is time a path or a container? I can't bear the thought of either.

Fiction invents where memoir records, writes Daniel Mendelsohn. Novels give us *a* truth, he says, memoirs give us *the* truth, or at least a piece of it. Whereas literature, and nonfiction in particular, often appears mired in questions of fact—as though that were the thing it's most qualified to give—the Canadian physician William Osler, one of the founding professors of the medical school at Johns Hopkins, once advised his students that fifty percent of what he told them would turn out to be wrong, he just didn't know *which* fifty percent. For Carl Sagan, too, science was an imperfect instrument, perpetually mired in error. Humans, he said, "may crave absolute certainty; they may aspire to it; they may pretend, as partisans of certain religions do, to have attained it. But the history of science… teaches that the most we can hope for is successive improvement in our understanding…an asymptotic approach to the Universe."

But you can see there's no order to it, this piling.

Some may find the idea that literature should, to varying degrees, approach the truth with the presumption of fact at odds with what they actually seek, and get, from it. In other fields, one may be forced to adopt the stance of the impartial observer, but it is profoundly the partiality of the speaker, in all its attendant forms, that literature embraces. Where other endeavors suppress the voice, writing revels in it and in the empathy and antipathy it allows. Example: a few years ago I started noticing a surfeit of "And yet" in my writing. I wondered what it meant as a rhetorical gesture, this hedge. I supposed it came from my love of the long sentence packed full of clauses, folding back on itself, again and again, the sentence that rocks and shakes as it rattles along the track of the syntax, rolling off toward some as yet unimagined Timbuktu. I have an affection for convolution that while wholly (or mostly) rational tends to assert a profound *nevertheless* at the center of my thinking, as though to say that nothing is so straightforward that it's free of uncertainty. For me, the direct path depends on the indirect one, which may be more direct for its indirection after all. I am in spite of myself: I am *notwithstanding*. This may be the truest confession I can offer, even if, as memoir, it's paltry fare.

Between the owl I heard on my run and my rendition of its call over breakfast.
Not long after moving back east, shortly after my thirty-third birthday, I drove into Philly for the day. It was my first time in the city, and after lunch I went down to the Race Street pier, where I sat staring at the rivets in the Ben Franklin Bridge. I knew Walt Whitman had spent the last twenty years of his life across the river in Camden, but beyond that there was nothing—no sense of the neglect that hangs over that city like a pall. As I was leaving I missed a turn and found myself crossing the bridge I had just been admiring. I had no cash to pay the toll, and the attendant in the booth only laughed from the core of her being when I explained what had happened. I was in for a treat, she said, sending me to look for a nearby ATM, but either her directions were bad or the streets addled me, as she might have known they would. I gradually worked my way through the abandoned buildings to the other side of the river I'd been sitting on a half-hour before. I came upon scores of people in cowboy hats, as though I had been teleported into some country town. What was this place, I thought, if not America itself, and when I spotted a confederate flag on

a parked pickup, Camden became, at least for a moment, a parable of the unreconstructed lives we were all contemptibly living. I also saw, more slowly, that it made for a good story, and that even the knowing attendant whose booth I returned to, money in hand, would probably—in her own way—retell it.

Art may not be real, but it makes us realize the world.
At the Brandt exhibit that day in New York, I fixated on a picture of Battersea Bridge. The year is 1939. In the foreground is the bank of the Thames: shadows, pebbles, and puddles cover three-quarters of the image. A smattering of boats rests in the water beneath the bridge, on just the other side of it. A barge moves along the river while one man appears to be rowing a much smaller vessel toward the bank. Above the bridge it's another world entirely. A Routemaster bus crosses in the upper right hand corner, and the Battersea Power Station, invisible below the line of the bridge, looms over the scene. The image captures a world that is at least two worlds, and though each is out of step with the other they are nonetheless coincident, as though superimposed. Brandt perceived in a flash what it has taken me years to confirm: I'm living at least two lives, probably more. The trick is to come up with an angle wide enough to capture them both. Nothing in the restaurant anyway was quite as I remembered, even if it hadn't changed. In some of its features it looked a little rundown, and I could tell from the demeanor of our waiter, from the conversation of our neighbors, that it was a place for putting on airs. That it always had been. The only difference was that now I was on the other side of that vanity, looking in at a conceit I was once part of and that, like it or not, was still a part of me.

That I am my own baseline.

Errors like these accrue over time, and whatever sense of precision one has adopted or internalized wears away. Weariness arises in its place, though my own is focused inward, less on the world than on my reading of it. I no longer feel that I am a perfectable center of gravity, even as I remain the calibration point for the world I experience. But then maybe precision isn't all it's cracked up to be. Maybe it's something you learn and then, if you're lucky, unlearn. As there are colors our eyes are not designed to see, sounds our ears are not designed to hear, so too are there dimensions of our lives that lie outside our abilities to perceive them.

Or else there is nothing but order.

Take the great European observatories, for example, which were founded, Dava Sobel writes, on the premise that astronomy was a means to an end: it was only necessary to chart the stars so that sailors might safely navigate the seas. The value in astronomy, from a mercantile point of view, was to enable the free flow of goods. Anything else that might come of it was pure gravy. That sidereal knowledge couldn't solve the problem of longitude may be the central irony at the heart of Sobel's book on the clockmaker who did, but it also speaks to larger ironies about how we proceed with our lives. How often, I wonder, are we blinded to less tangible gains by more tangible goals? How often does one form of living, or knowing, preclude another?

Through and between and around and beyond.

Notwithstanding sounds to the modern ear like three words joined into one, but here *with* is an Old English prefix meaning *away* or *against*, as in the root word, *withstand*. It probably came into English through the French use of a Latin legal term. By granting a *non obstante*, a king could exempt a person from whatever law he had broken, but to *withstand* something is to resist or oppose it, successfully so. I can withstand my temptation to have a beer right now, as it is only nine thirty in the morning. But add to the word "the ordinary adverb of negation," and I'll walk down to the kitchen, open the fridge and grab a beer, time of day *notwithstanding*. What had been incontrovertible—i.e., that I don't drink in the morning—gets turned on its head just this once. Indeed, what was incontrovertible remains so even in this case: that I'm drinking beer this morning doesn't mean I normally do or ever will again. It's a word of qualification, yes, but even more a word of exception. It indicates a deviation from the general rule. Applied to the simple phrase *I am*, it suggests that whatever the laws are that govern the self, either from within or without, they don't apply. Or, again, that they do but are temporarily held in suspension.

Do I want my writing to redeem me? Do you?

I became aware of myself, in New York, as a problem to which there is no solution. At the center of my experience lies the caveat that my lens is warped in a way I don't exactly like or even understand, and it may be that my sudden desire, while crossing the Bow Bridge, to return to the Café Luxembourg was an impulse to reorient it. If I could observe the place objectively, through the distance of a decade—or the framework of a bridge—it might also be possible to measure the distance between my earlier impression and my present one, so as to produce a yardstick for my distortion. Because the past is not a mountain one has climbed, from whose summit one can say, having surveyed the landscape from above, that either it wasn't as bad as it felt or that whatever has happened was worth it. There I was in the restaurant, enjoying the wine, the soft lighting, the large mirrors along the walls. In their reflections I saw how I might embrace contradiction as a matter of first principles, how I might situate myself not at any point along the yardstick of my perceptions but as the span itself. The readings are multiple. They negate one another. And in another year, or another decade, my impressions will have changed again completely, in which case the yardstick too will have changed, and what I might have mistaken at any point along the way for objectivity will have become yet another notch on the spectrum of the possible.

Couldn't one make the argument—am I making it now?
It may be that a person desires the exception, seeks a vehicle for its fulfillment—the vehicle, say, of confession. It may be that the impulse to confess has less to do with exhibitionism or self-involvement than with a need to push the limits of the self beyond their breaking point, to write a self that moves beyond the laws governing its sociability, to turn the whole apparatus inside-out, inhibition *notwithstanding*.

That the self is no less of a fiction, the stories it comprises inventions.
In the city again months later—it was then May of 2013—I was surprised to see the Brandt show still hanging. It had been raining off and on for three days, but I had been walking quite a lot, and falling asleep in the hotel, I pictured the shape of the day's movements. It appeared, from above, as a mammoth abstraction, though with a centripetal order to it, an invisible center that might be crossed but not inhabited. In the morning, I walked north from the museum into the park, hoping for some sun, but

it was only that evening in the train when I finally saw it setting over New Jersey. I had watched, in the meantime, a film in which the characters do little other than walk and talk, the third in a series whose previous installment I saw nine years earlier in the same theater. That time produces such feedback as a consequence of its passing may be nothing new, but when I immediately grasped that the picture of Battersea Bridge was one of the least interesting in the show, I was struck by how little I understood this particular loop when I entered it, how little I understand it even now. I could only see that even over a short period my impressions had shifted, and as I lingered over Brandt's late images of sand and skin, abstractions of rock and bone, I couldn't say where these images would lead me, whether I would return to them changed or whether, over time, they would change me. Struggling to make my way through the frenzied lobby, it occurred to me they might be—like time itself—bridges to nowhere.

In which physical sense is briefly supplanted.

I look back at what I've written, but as I read through these pages each paragraph pulses, as though it were observing me. I have been here for what feels like years. Hours have gone by. It has only been a few minutes, a few seconds even, that I've been here. I don't know what to make of this place, where no moment is so static that it cannot dissolve, no moment so evanescent it won't become tangible once more. I'm less bothered by this uncertainty than by the errors I know I have yet to commit in reconciling my experience with my understanding, my anything with my everything. The contours rise and fall, the cadences swell and shift, but this is no bridge, no street corner, no pile of paragraphs I'm standing on.

The idea had been to see the cherry blossoms, but either they were past their peak or the spring was so protracted they never reached it. We took our son to see the dinosaurs instead, or rather—but how to explain this to a four-year-old—we took him to see the models created from molds scientists had made of their bones. Afterwards, we walked down to the Lincoln Memorial to have lunch on its steps, which were packed densely enough, as was the whole area, to drive us into the trees on the periphery. That was just as well. The whole experience—flowers, dinosaurs, memorials—had aroused my ambivalence, and the longer we sat there that feeling transformed into open hostility. I recoiled from the overblown trappings of Athenian democracy, or was it Athenian ruin?

I remember feeling differently when, at thirteen, my parents brought my brother and me here as part of our civic education. It wasn't that the trip inspired any real patriotism, nor was it precisely intended to, but I suppose I felt the paternalism of the place as a comfort, not a menace. I didn't yet see that the versions of history I had been spoonfed had been written by the victors, and that to someone looking back on first seeing the ships arrive off the coast of Hispaniola, Massachusetts, or Virginia—ships that must have appeared as though from some alien civilization—the course of history could only read as a progressive disintegration.

Walking the area with our son, it felt fitting that the memorial I most admired was built just outside the mall proper, as though the dominant version of the American myth meant a peripheral place for justice. "Injustice anywhere is a threat to justice everywhere," read one inscription in the marble: "We are caught in an inescapable network of mutuality, tied in a single garment of destiny. Whatever affects one directly, affects all indirectly." Although in my thirties I take King's words as a credo, I realize how absent his sentiment was from that civic education. Staring up at Lincoln twenty years earlier, or running my fingers along the names of the war dead, it didn't occur to me that I was a political site, a small but vital node in King's "network of mutuality."

In the homogeny of 1990s West Michigan, there was little reason for a straight white kid to become a site of resistance. I grew up with a variety of privilege that meant, at least in my hometown, my skin, gender, and sexuality didn't immediately politicize my body. Or rather, I didn't *feel* politicized, even though, as I know now, it's impossible for a body not to be. Had I been transplanted at thirteen to parts of DC beyond the tourist trail, I would not have had the same luxury. My body would have marked me in a way that it never had at home.

That could be why, in retrospect, I admire those kids who took up the gauntlet in spite of their apparent exemption. For whatever reason, they must have felt King's sense of mutuality much earlier than I did. Either that or some part of their lives had incited a rebellion that would never be quelled, only stoked, by the comforts that kept the rest of us quiet. I'll never forget the sight of one of these kids, a scrawny guy named Marc, wearing a flowered dress and playing, at a school dance, a cover of Nirvana's "Rape Me" with his band. The administrators were appalled, but most of us were simply confused. The sexual politics in the cafeteria that night didn't conform to anything anyone in the room had been taught. We lived in what is still one of the most conservative congressional districts in the country, and at least as I remember it, the assistant principal cut the power before the song was finished.

It was undoubtedly some version of my admiration for Marc that re-emerged in March of this year, not long before our trip to DC, when I learned that a nineteen-year-old Tunisian woman named Amina Tyler had posted two photos to her Facebook page. In the first, she had written the words "Fuck your morals" across her bare chest; in the second, this time in Arabic, "My body belongs to me, and is not the source of anyone's honor." The response was severe. By her own account, Tyler was drugged by her family, whisked away to a secret location, and there subjected to virginity tests. One prominent cleric publicly demanded she be stoned to death.

If the photos had been sexual, it wouldn't have made for international news, but in asserting her body as the site of an informed political self, she raised the ire of conservatives, who saw in her liberation from the abstractions of modesty the possibility of a vicious contagion. Tyler meant to reclaim the body and to begin thereby to shape the nature of the state. At least on this level, conservatives were right to feel alarmed. Her breasts were absolutely a threat.

Weeks later, groups of European women protested in solidarity, writing similar slogans across their own bare torsos, and Tyler's viral gesture adopted a physical form. In the photographs that wound up back in the ether, many of the women stand assertively, even aggressively, feet shoulder-length apart, one arm raised upward in a fist. In some pictures, protestors are being dragged away from in front of embassies, mosques, monuments, and, in a photo taken weeks later, Angela Merkel and Vladimir Putin. In one dramatic shot, an older man kicks a protestor, whose face is covered in a pseudo-jihadist scarf.

The organizing group calls itself Femen, and the rhyme with semen is as provocative as the nudity central to its strategy. It may be because the female body is simultaneously an object of desire and the site par excellence of repression that it works as a tool of protest, but while critics argue that Femen's tactics are hypocritical, there's more to it than reveling in surfaces: in revealing themselves the protestors unveil a pervasive unease with the body, a general preference for a concealment that is at once domineering and titillating. Remove what is either the ruse of ornamentation or true tyranny over the body and the response, as Femen and Tyler prove, is dramatic. In a sea of burqas and business suits—even in a sea of bikinis—a naked form is nearly anarchic. And though one can claim that these protests do nothing to advance women, such arguments may miss the point. All demonstrations are symbolic, as John Berger writes. They do not represent political action as much as they dramatize the power the demonstrators lack. It isn't to solve inequality in one fell swoop that the Femen activists remove their clothing: it is to dramatize that inequality— to make a scene of the body, rather than an abstraction of it.

The cherry blossoms came and went, but Femen stuck around all summer. The group presented a dilemma I had long been interested in: justice, as it pertains to the body. I had also seen, on one of those weekends in March or April, Harmony Korine's film *Spring Breakers*, and it, too, stuck around all summer. I spent an inordinate amount of time arguing about the film, which had become entwined, in my mind, with Femen. Where other cultures blatantly repress their young, I remember saying (or trying to say) one night while various kids, including our son, were propped in front of the TV, ours infantilizes them, reducing them to gleaming torsos and pleasure-seeking naïfs, and in this country in particular, repression often goes by the insidious name of *freedom*. Take *Girls Gone Wild*, for instance, in which the subjects do not shed submission along with their clothing but rather adopt another version of the male gaze.

The title of Korine's film also seems to say it all. But instead of bare bodies and easy living, Korine delivers a fantasia on gender, race, and violence—an allegory with characters named Candy and Faith, characters for whom the body is hardly a body any more, or rather it is *only* body:

little or no self persists here, only its (bomb-) shell. It is the purely superficial body to which the culture prostrates itself continuously. It is the body made meat, and as it has been rendered into the shape of desire, so it renders all it touches—or that touches it—into extensions of an unquenchable want. That the sex *Spring Breakers* appears to promise never comes to fruition is also in perfect keeping with a principle common to much pop culture wherein pornographic poses are adopted but not fulfilled. In Korine's hands, these empty sexual gestures become ironic stagings both of what we have been trained to desire and how this desire is purposefully thwarted. Although the young women in the film may have been shaped by the male gaze, in the final act this gaze turns on itself and it is as though, to borrow a line from the French collective Tiqqun, "we witness an ironic epilogue in which the 'male sex' becomes both the victim and the object of its own alienated desire."

Whether Korine's film is a confection, a prophecy, or a verdict was the source of some debate on those summer nights when we tried to tranquilize our kids to talk a little longer, but it is in the film's final violent scenes, I maintained, that the costs of infantilization, which is at root about control, stand out in stark relief. The projections come home to roost, and everybody falls victim to the apotheosis of the bikini-clad blonde—no one more so than the black bodies that line the grounds of the mansion at which, near the end of the film, the "heroines" unload their dainty semi-automatics. Those bodies that conform least to the dominant paradigm are sacrificed to it. In the end, we're back at the beginning in some sense, at the lecture the two female leads are attending. The professor is speaking about civil rights during World War II. The girls are not paying any attention.

In itself, the body is neither moral nor political. It is a field on which morality, like politics, is played, a screen onto which it is projected. Moreover, the body remains when the play has ended—not as a blank space, as something to be filled (or drained), but as a figure whose nakedness defines its function. Put another way, fashion is moral in a manner the bare body never could be: in wearing the burqa, for example, a woman suppresses her body in favor of her belief or, alternately, her modesty. Here, to dress is also to subdue the power of the female form, which, this thinking holds, wreaks havoc. Either women can't control their sexuality or men can't control themselves from temptation; in either case, it is as though we need protection from the body, as though there were no greater threat than its display. But if the wearer of the burqa reveals her morality, it is not necessarily the case—as hardliners of all stripes would have you believe—that the wearer of the bikini reveals her amorality, for the bikini may be less of a proxy for emancipation than an emblem of our own skewed sexual politics. It may be a more palatable variation of the fetishization that elsewhere insists upon the body's complete concealment. It may dazzle, but what it most reveals is, paradoxically, what it demands on concealing.

That the body has become both the province and indeed the basis of power is the premise of Tiqqun's *Preliminary Materials for a Theory of the Young-Girl*. "Youth and Femininity," they argue, "abstracted and recoded… find themselves raised to the rank of the ideal regulators of…the Imperial citizenry." The figure of the Young-Girl, write Tiqqun, is an instrument in the ongoing total war waged by capitalism on the people who keep it afloat, an invisible war dependent on "the molecular diffusion of constraint into everyday life." Empire extends to the body, and the struggle becomes "to render oneself compatible" with that imperialism—to wear the burqa or, conversely, to work on one's bikini's body, so as to reify social control. We tell ourselves we are working on our appearances, but appearances are working on us, and in the process our bodies become the picture of dominion, the embodiment of forces that can only express themselves through us. In place of the shitting, bleeding, stinking one, we assert the body-as-abstraction, as lure, as "the eradication of all alterity."

It's now autumn, but the brightness in the leaves has yet to arrive. At a party a few weeks ago, most had mixed feelings about the mild weather, which meant the women were still wearing summer dresses well into October and the men were in shorts and t-shirts. Sitting on our friends' sunny patio, I made the mistake of bringing up *Spring Breakers* once again. Among us there were those who, respectively, saw irony, anarchy, and exploitation in it. The talk turned to Amina Tyler, and though one vocal critic of the film said she mostly agreed with me about Femen—that there was something noble in it—she was suspicious of the protestors because, in this instance, their praises were being sung by a man.

She has a point. What right do I have to make pronouncements about the experiences of bodies so unlike my own, bodies that have, unlike mine, been aggressively politicized in various ways practically since conception? What right do I have to address categories of which I am not myself a member? How can I not be blinded by the prejudices inherent in my culture, my upbringing, my way of being in the world? These strike me as entirely reasonable objections. And yet King's words come back to me: shouldn't I have as much of a stake in Amina Tyler's liberation, or nearly so, as Amina herself? Isn't the question of justice at its core really a question of my responsibility for and to her burdens, the burdens of everyone who has not had the privilege of a life spent in a globally dominant demographic?

In the hallway outside my office, I bump into a colleague who has recently sent me a wonderful essay about physical space. I tell her that it helped me solve a problem I was having with another essay, a structural hurdle that was giving me headaches at night. I say that I am now working on an essay—having put the other one to rest, thanks to her—about activism and the body, but that I've once again run into a roadblock. At issue, I say, is my place in it all. I cannot imagine the circumstances under which I would lay my body on the line the way Amina Tyler did. She says she has no trouble imagining them, either for me or for her. When it comes to fracking, to the Keystone Pipeline, she would put herself in harm's way. Later, I wonder what this might look like. I imagine us drinking quarts of contaminated water at the site of a proposed well, or donning gas masks and chaining ourselves to bulldozers. I wonder what it means that I have less trouble imagining my colleague doing these things, but that in the meantime I'm the one writing about them.

Even as someone opposed to both fracking and tar sands oil, I'm still not convinced by my own stake in the issues. I have difficulty placing my body in their path, in conceiving of it as a contaminated site, or potentially so, and I realize that this is where the true failure of my civic education rears its head. Growing up as and where I did, I never learned to feel the body politic in the body proper. I was insulated from the consequences of identity, and as such I have trouble tuning into the issues that might incite me to action. I may feel disgusted by fracking wells, but at a remove. It is an intellectual disgust, one from which, as a body, I'm cut off.

This may be why, in retrospect, I did not fly to New York City in October 2011 as the Occupy protests gathered steam, even though it had immediately occurred to me to drop everything and join them. I understood that the plutocracy is out of control, but my outrage was tempered by my reason, as it often is with people like me. I was willing to send money, via a Nicaraguan social justice website, but I was unwilling to sacrifice my livelihood. I had the dual privileges of my outrage and my well-being, the latter tempering the former, almost by design.

Then the protests went viral, with distant sympathizers telling their stories of corporate malfeasance and personal misfortune, adding at the end, "I am the 99%." These were posted online by the thousands, each person holding her placard in front of a computer camera, which often had the ironic, if unintentional, effect of partially obscuring the person who held it. The stories, too, tended to obviate the subject: it mattered most that what one wrote was on message, that it kept to the script. Again, my temptation to participate was modulated by something else—in this case, my suspicion that these stories were less rhetorically effective than they might have been.

When I saw the Tyler photos, a year and a half later, it struck me that she had taken the gesture a step further: her message did not mediate her body, or vice versa. Her message *was* her body, and her body her message. While it may not be the case that the virtual Occupiers would have been more effective if, like Tyler, their 99% stories had been written on bare bodies, in obscuring themselves with their signs they may have garbled their substance, defusing their power at the site of its mobilization, muting themselves in the moment they spoke.

If we need some mechanism to project ourselves and our causes into true visibility, Tyler's stroke of brilliance was to realize she had just such an apparatus: herself. The challenge she continues to raise is how to embody resistance, how to live one's cause in, or with, one's body *and* in the context (not *at the expense*) of one's life. Because to shield that life, to conceal that body, is to disarm it. Divorced from the corporeal and the quotidian, one can only be as others are, and these disembodied abstractions become easy prey for empire, which *deals* in abstractions. As concept replaces contour, the body's boundaries are replaced by the tragedy of their obfuscation, and though that tragedy may be ironized to some effect (as in Korine's *Spring Breakers*) it is difficult to tell, in the desert—or beach sand—of our alienation, where that irony begins and ends.

It is in the nature of a demonstration, Berger writes, to provoke violence upon itself, and the degree to which the state responds with violence is an indication of how serious a threat the demonstration is to its power: compare the eviction from Zuccoti Park, or the infamous pepper-spraying at UC-Davis, to the violence provoked by Tyler's breasts or, for that matter, by the Arab Spring itself. As of this writing, more than a hundred thousand people have been killed in the Syrian civil war; in Egypt and Libya, as the Mubarak and Gaddafi regimes were in their final throes, the state responded by imprisoning, torturing, and murdering the opposition.

One would like to see the absence of violence in response to Occupy as a product of our democratic values, but the truth may be that the movement expressed, as Slavoj Žižek has written, "a spirit of revolt without revolution." It was, at best, an exercise in consciousness-raising; at worst, it was little more self-congratulatory than buying a "Starbucks cappuccino where 1% goes for the third world troubles." In place of actual liberation, there was the illusion of it, permitted just long enough for it to appear that there was real opposition and debate, when there was neither. Consider the misnomer, Occupy Wall Street: no one was camping out on the trading floor. It was, and continues to be, business as usual.

In some ways, Occupy was a tremendous success—more so than any Femen protest to date. For weeks, the demonstrators, both in person and online, put on a great show. The problem with the performance was not that it remained primarily a dramatization, but that it may only have been a form of theater to begin with, the theater of disenfranchisement. The protestors never represented a threat to the state, as was proven by the state's slow and quiet response.

While it may be possible to have revolt without revolution, it's impossible to have revolution without risk. Mohamed Bouazizi—the Tunisian street vendor whose self-immolation became the catalyst for the Arab Spring—had his wares confiscated. Already deeply in debt, he could no longer make a living. On the surface of it, he risked everything (his life) because he had nothing (his life) left to lose. For him—and for how many others?—the boundary between everything and nothing became dangerously blurred at the site of the only something that remained to him: his body. Bouazizi's tragedy may not be Tyler's, but for both to act is to wager the body, to assert the something of that body against the nothingness (the everything-in-nothing) it is so often reduced to, in various repressive ways.

This urgency propelled the initial Egyptian revolution, but it's worth noting, considering the questions at play here, that it didn't ensure its success. It could just be that few revolutions turn out that well, but the constitution of the first democratically elected parliament was most striking for the way it censored parties that were vital to Mubarak's overthrow, namely liberals and women. In a country in which, according to the journalist Mona Eltahawy, 90% of ever-married women have undergone Female Genital Mutilation, is it any coincidence that only eight seats in the 508-member parliament were held by women? What we mistake for liberation is often a mechanism for averting it, and it is, in that connection, more than a passing curiosity that in the United States women fill only a fifth of the seats in the Senate and slightly less than that in the House.

I don't know whatever happened to Marc, the would-be Kurt Cobain from my high school, so I can't say whether these days he's still dressing in drag or whether he's now a corporate accountant with a smattering of kids and a house in the suburbs. Maybe it's both. As an emblem of revolution the executive in drag may be a little uninspiring, but such a person, if he exists, may be occupying his life on a profound level. I wonder about all the people for whom any demonstration is merely an outgrowth of the way they live their lives. This may be the truest occupation, in every sense: rather than the message mediating the life, or vice versa, the message becomes the life, and the life the message.

I cannot claim to have done this with anything like consistency or rigor, nor can I claim to have done anything as daring as Marc or Amina Tyler, and if throughout these pages I've been asking what it means for a body to become a political site (without becoming prey or pawn), it is in part because I realize what a poor one my own has made. What I've struggled with here, what I'm struggling with still, is that there is only the sketchiest map for the solidarity I'm interested in. Worse yet, the route through the territory is bounded by the opposing perils of privilege and desperation, and both action and inaction can become detours into foolishness.

But I am also beginning to feel, somewhere in my bones, that any body is every body, that what is done to one is done to all. When, for instance, I read the story of Daisy Coleman—the Maryville, Missouri, teenager who was first raped by the scion of a prominent local family and whose own family was then tormented by the town—it occurs to me that, to protest the mysterious dismissal of charges against her assailant, engineered no doubt by his powerful relatives, I might take and post online a naked photo of myself with the words "This is not an instrument of rape" written on my abdomen.

That this is almost the last thing I will actually do strikes me as a sign of the complacency that is the sine qua non of my demographic. I say this with no more self-loathing than necessary. Instead, I would like to see in that self-diagnosis a prescription against the variety of political awareness Joan Didion compared, more than forty years ago, to the movies. "Things 'happen' in motion pictures," she wrote. "There is always a resolution, a strong cause-effect dramatic line, and to perceive the world in those terms is to assume an ending for every social scenario." More defiantly, she pointed to "the particular vanity of perceiving social life as a problem to be solved by the good will of individuals." History, she suggested, doesn't progress in an orderly, elegant fashion. It's a messy matter, full of sacrifice and surrender. Or, as Mona Eltahawy writes of Egypt, "Until the rage shifts from the oppressors in our presidential palaces to the oppressors on our streets and in our homes"—the oppressors, I might add, in ourselves—"our revolution has not even begun."

The game starts sluggishly. After spelling *greet* for fourteen points, I've used all my vowels. Over the next few rounds I spell words thick with consonants, leaching off those my opponent plays. She spells *towns*. She spells *grieve*. There is a logic to these words, taken together, but I look hopelessly at my tiles. I pick up the *q* but have nowhere to play it.

*

As a freshman in high school I was assigned a career report in my sixth hour English class, and on May 27, 1994, I turned in the five-pager I now have before me, "Bridging History and the News." Divided into four sections—"Overview," "Quality of Character," "Skills, Talents, Education," and the bizarrely titled "Obstacles to Success, Losses"—the essay is a comparison piece: I establish John Gunther as a model writer and then outline the ways I am like and unlike him. My choice of Gunther was as arbitrary as my high school library was quaint, and as a result the essay is full of adolescent absurdities, such as my claims that Gunther wrote his books "all by himself" and that, as though I were talking about Joyce, what he attempted "may never be accomplished again." But for all of its faults, the essay contains some unintentional wisdom. Although I declared that there are always more writers than there is work, I believed my dedication would help me succeed. "Mr. Gunther had a hard job," I wrote at fourteen, "but he loved it."

*

My opponent will be sixty-two this year. In recent years she has dealt with a failing father and mother-in-law, whose long senescences have created considerable stress. In late January of 2013, and in consultation with various doctors, she and her siblings decided to remove the medications keeping their father alive and to allow death to take its course. It was soon nearly April—holy week, in fact—and he was still among us. My opponent was playing a lot right then, in the moments, I imagine, that the waiting became unbearable. It's very sad, she told me, but words cannot show how it hurts.

*

The report was an assignment, mostly, like dissecting a frog, minus the formaldehyde stink. I remember my teacher, whoever it was (I can't pinpoint a face or a name), telling me that it was a tough life, being a writer—hard to make a living at it, for one thing. I wasn't then in the habit of writing and wouldn't be for many years, nor was I a particularly active reader, but like so many things in my life I don't remember it being much of a choice. Nothing else appealed to me—doctor, lawyer, electrician—as nothing else has really appealed to me since. And yet I don't precisely earn a living as a writer. I never have and likely never will. My teaching and writing intersect but they are not the same, and I often have to remind myself of the difference between my job and my vocation, lest teaching supplant writing and writing slide practically and semantically into avocation. What that career report taught me more than twenty years ago was that writing both is and isn't a job. We talk about reading a writer's *work*, but it isn't labor in the common economic sense we mean. I'm not getting paid to sit here, but that I do so incessantly, out of all sense of proportion, speaks to me more of compulsion, of mania, of *pre*-occupation, and, in another way, of play.

*

In the classic game of Scrabble, the twenty-six letters of the alphabet are distributed, to varying frequencies, across ninety-eight tiles, and in the version I played as a kid these came in a faux-velvet bag along with two blanks. Then as now, a game with only two players will last an average of fifteen to twenty rounds, at the end of which the tiles, progressively emptied from the bag, and temporarily fixed into place on the board, return to it, ready for the next game to begin. Letters that mean everything one moment mean nothing the next.

*

Over the years I've applied for dozens of academic jobs, probably hundreds. I've flown to conferences. I've flown to campuses. I took first one visiting position, then another. I sometimes marvel at my perseverance, and at the mostly unexamined goal of acquiring a job from which I would never, with any luck, be dismissed. I have operated in blind observance of a system I have internalized to such an extent that I confuse its aims, means, and methods with my own. During my first year on the job market, I cast a wide net and got a single interview. I remember feeling silly about flying halfway across the country to sit in a hotel room for thirty minutes with people who had flown even farther, teachers and writers who, in the hours before and after my allotted timeslot would lob questions at other eager job seekers. The whole thing amounted to an exercise in waste, but I was a captive participant. And even though my son had been born only two weeks earlier, in late December I got on a plane to San Francisco not so much to attend the 124th annual meeting of the Modern Language Association but to lurk in its shadows. I made dinner plans with friends, also in town for interviews, and after dropping my bags at the hotel (misleadingly named the Good) dashed to meet them. California was deep in the throes of a budget crisis, and I almost immediately received a ticket for jaywalking. I tried to dispel any sense of omen by telling myself they were drumming up revenue, but the interview didn't go well the next day. I was young and inexperienced, and the poet and playwright who interviewed me didn't take me any more seriously than I took them. Or no, that isn't quite right. I took the whole thing too seriously, as though my life depended on it. At the time I believed in the story of my *ever-greater* success. My ambition had the power of a truth.

*

In the wholly derivative but superficially altered version I play on my phone, there are four additional tiles and different letter distributions. The colored bonus spaces form a diamond pattern on the board, whereas in the classic version they form a large X. This changes the shape of the play, as in Scrabble you stretch toward the corners and in Words with Friends less so. Knowing that might yield some reward, if not in the game then outside it, some insight into what it means to stake a claim to some small portion of the universe, but what matters most in the patterns is their change over time, how, regardless of the board, no two games are alike.

*

Each year I've applied to fewer jobs. I've had interviews, though not always the ones I expected. I've had offers, too, though not always the ones I wanted. There have been moments of doubt, times when the operation felt like a doomed campaign: an uninspiring candidate running on a predictable platform. For a short while, I even considered doing something other than teaching and cast about for alternatives. I applied to jobs more or less at random, and unsurprisingly, given that I was aiming in the dark, nearly no one responded. Only one of these forays yielded an interview, for a technical writing job at a medical software company in Wisconsin. The day before the interview, I roamed Madison on foot, stopping in bookstores, the local museum of contemporary art, and the terrace Frank Lloyd Wright designed for Lake Monona, which—because of the rallies against the state's governor, Scott Walker, who was then stripping teachers' unions of their collective bargaining power—was strangely abandoned. I encountered only one person in the entire place, an old woman who encouraged me to look around but who didn't appear to work there any more than I did. In the morning, I took a shuttle bus to the corporate campus with a handful of other interviewees. There were even more people interviewing when we arrived, mostly for other jobs: software developers, project managers, salesmen. The company had a finely tuned system for shuffling us into and out of one session or another. It was an orderly insanity that owed much to the assembly line. I flew back to Denver that afternoon, and later in the week the company called to offer me the job. The money was barely more than what I was earning as an adjunct, but the real reason for turning the offer down, as I almost immediately did, was that I hadn't wanted the job in the first place. It was an answer to the problem of my ambition, but it wasn't the right one.

*

Years passed. There were more interviews, more visits, and by February of 2014 I was waiting for an offer I was certain I would get, an offer for the kind of job I'd been working toward, a job I was lucky enough to actually want. But as I waited for the phone call, another came one night, out of the blue. It was an offer for a job at a school where I had interviewed the year before. The person who had accepted it first delayed her start then backed out entirely. The timing, depending on how you looked at it, could not have been either better or worse. *Better* because I suddenly possessed a leverage I had been lacking: I could return to the other school, the job I wanted, with an offer on the table. I could say *the clock is ticking— please make up your mind.* On the other hand, I now had an offer for a job I hadn't particularly wanted when I interviewed for it. There had been too many red flags, from the decked out Mustang that met me at the airport to the surly department chair who wore a polo shirt with the school's name emblazoned on it to dinner. Publically, I responded with enthusiasm— privately, with skepticism. I wrote to the other school. They were working on it, they said. A week went by. I wrote to them again. Still working, they said. Hang in there. Meanwhile, I was negotiating the terms of the other offer, dragging the process out as much as possible, though I knew at this point I was almost certainly my first choice's second or third, that the delay was due to their negotiations with another candidate. A second week went by. Time was running out, I told them. Soon I would have to sign the papers.

*

We progress little by little, action followed by reaction, but while I sometimes feel I'm directing things, there's no telling what my opponent will do, how her moves—and our random drawing of letters—will shape mine. The outcome is never apparent from inside the game. Strategies have only short-term effects: keeping your opponent from big scores while maximizing your own. No tactic can be directed toward the shape of the game as a whole, which is only ever a product of the responses that comprise it. To *scrabble* for something is to struggle for it, to scratch or scramble to reach it, as though one were sliding, or falling, or being whisked down a river, frantically searching with one's hands for a firm grip, something, anything, to hold onto.

*

Two days later, I got the call. They had offered the job to someone else initially, but she had turned it down after dragging her feet for two weeks. They acknowledged the timing was terrible, but what could they do? My interview had been excellent, they said, but the other candidate brought more experience, more cachet. I was now in a difficult position, I said, and wasn't sure about the ethics of what they were asking. But yes, I would consider it. This is a good problem to have, I thought. Others I knew had wound up in both pleasant and miserable situations because it was the only offer they received. Good problem or not, it took a toll. It was a dreamy job in, to my wife's mind, a less-than-dreamy location. She didn't want to go. And so the choice changed shape. I was no longer deciding between one job and another: I was choosing between a job and a marriage, or so it felt. Having already accepted the first offer, I begrudgingly turned down the second, citing the bad timing, my wife's preferences, what I said— without exactly believing—was better for my family. I hadn't wanted the first job, but everyone agreed it was my only choice, and coming as it had as a complete surprise it was almost, some said, like providence.

*

Off of *feet* I spell *qi*. It's a triple word score, and I pick up another five points for the *if* I play with the vowel. We discovered this answer to the problem of the *q* early on; now the circulating life force in Chinese medicine is a regular feature of our games. My opponent dispatched me in the previous one by spelling it twice, vertically and horizontally. It was a stellar play at the end of a tight match. While it's still early in this one, *qi* has broken things open a bit. My opponent will need a big play in the next couple rounds to bring us even again. Lucky for her, I'm lousy with *n*'s and *l*'s.

*

I should have been happy with the outcome. My dedication had paid off, and after years of striving I could finally relax into my life a little. But I wasn't happy. Not at all. I couldn't see myself in Florida and didn't want to leave the comparatively good thing I already had. I inhabited a depression in the shape of the Sunshine State. I read about the sinkholes common to the area and metaphorized the peninsula into one. Having pushed for this job, though mostly in opposition to the other one, my wife was no happier. I understood. I'd given her two options, but she hadn't wanted either. Some weeks went by. I taught, browsed the real estate listings, and sometime that spring, when I could string a few hours together, I picked up Elizabeth Kolbert's *The Sixth Extinction*. In its penultimate chapter, I read a profile of Svante Pääbo, "the father of paleogenetics," who notes that archaic humans and Neanderthals never ventured "out on the ocean where you don't see land." Only fully modern humans have done that, and Pääbo's take is, whether for glory or curiosity, there's "some madness there"—the same madness that drives us now to Mars and beyond. Kolbert calls it our "Faustian restlessness," and looking back that spring at the trajectory of my life, I felt that some version of Pääbo's madness had been with me all along. I had lived at eleven different addresses in just over a decade, and that summer I was planning to move once more. How much of my life had been spent this way, I wondered, jumping from place to place, in anticipation of things to come? From the beginning any life can have only one conclusion, but we still search continuously for better endings than the scripted one. (What a marvelous story heaven is, an ingenious solution to an intractable narrative problem.) I place my life in time, and I imagine resolutions to the plots and subplots I weave out of the material I know best: myself. I seek endings, I seek beginnings, but most of all I prepare to cast off again, discarding the past, in search of the future.

*

Some games are decidedly compact, with all the letters bunched to one side. In others, the play progresses in tendrils, curving out or looping back. But it's often the negative space that defines the picture once it's complete: the holes where the game couldn't go stand out against the places it did. Winning, in this light, is a matter of wresting a place from oblivion, of carving out a space from the tiniest of footholds. Emptiness is the natural state of the board, broken only by the arbitrary imposition of that initial pearl of a word, and though it's obvious that the board would remain empty were it not for the game, it still feels profound that, set against the blankness of the playing field, the impetus to begin means everything. Or almost everything: the letters move, singly or in bunches, from the grab-bag to the tile racks to the board. Their number is finite, and eventually their source is exhausted. Sometimes the board feels full before all the tiles are played, and you stuff the letters wherever you can. Sometimes there's room to play more rounds, and while it then feels the game ends prematurely, it's a reminder that finitude defines the play as much as variation gives it meaning.

*

The thing about restlessness is that it can blind you to what's at hand. That might even be its purpose. Because what's at hand isn't always pleasant, and sometimes it's easier just to turn away. I've been staring at the first sentence of this paragraph for the past two days, for instance. I stand up. Walk downstairs. Get a few pretzels and almonds. Play a word (*alb*) on my phone. The sentence itself is making me restless. I don't want to expand on it, or don't know how. So I pour a glass of water, check my email, play another word (*relent*). I'm clearly lacking in discipline, but I don't want to face these pages, what they represent. And lucky me, I have all these distractions at my fingertips. I wonder about those Polynesians setting out into the unknown in their long canoes, or Columbus in his carrack: what were they avoiding? We talk about exploration in terms of progress and ambition, but suppose we have it backwards. Suppose what Columbus first discovered when he set foot on Hispaniola was Columbus. For a while, he might have imagined he'd found something new, but how quickly the old world impressed itself, its terms and conditions displacing those it had only just met. Between that sentence and this one, I've done it again, playing yet another word (*pout*). I had thought, prior to shifting focus, that I ought to record what it is I'm facing or not facing in this moment, other than restlessness itself. What exactly did I hope to find in Florida? What did I hope to escape?

*

Several rounds later we are in much the same position as before. I have held onto my early lead without it becoming a blowout. Our words have been serviceable if uninspired. The algorithms that serve as digital judges have, questionably in my opinion, accepted my opponent's *rax*, but that's the limit of their eccentricity. Words like *fret* and *slam* and *hone* predominate. I have two *o*'s, two *a*'s, two *d*'s, and a blank tile. I settle for playing *oat* alongside *hit*, which also gives me *ha* and *git*. I feel I've wasted my blank, that little chameleon. I would have liked to spell *doodads*, in homage to the portable chunks of circuitry and plastic we use to play, but what one can do so often constrains what one wants to do.

*

The other day I got a call from the son-in-law of one my father's friends. Let's call him *you*. You had finished a PhD at an Ivy League school and now couldn't find a job. I sympathized, I said, though you had only been at it for a year. *Call me again in three*, I thought, but then you admitted you'd had a breakdown and were taking pills for the anxiety. I understood. The process itself is anxiety-producing, the way it situates a person in time. I had a soccer coach once, when I was twelve or thirteen, who told me my problem was that my head moved faster than my feet. For five long years, I told you, I've had my eyes on where I'll be next September or thirty Septembers from now. But a person can't live in the future any more than he can live in the past. It's hard enough to live in the present, which may be why we spend so much time looking forward or back, and which may, in turn, be why we need those pills. The future nettles us. We stare into it, trying to fathom what it holds, but it's always an abyss. At a day's distance, we get a reasonable reading, less so at a week. A month is barely an outline, if even. A year from now, the following fall—at that point, the words mean nothing.

*

I rack up a triple-word score on *jet*. She follows with *jive*, minimizing the damage, but still my lead is growing. The game may be getting away from her. I spell *adapt* and find the *z* among my tiles.

*

The job I wanted all those years—it's the job we all want—is defined by its security. Nice work if you can get it, but there's no guarantee. Careers can derail, lives turn sour. For one reason or another, one might not want to stay. A friend wrote to me: if you'll be looking for a new job in three years, then the security this one offers isn't security at all. Besides, my friend wrote, are you a teacher who writes or a writer who teaches? I had been working contingently for years, I said, and was sick of feeling like I didn't know where next year's paychecks would come from. I thought that if I could take care of the future, I could focus on the present, but all that time I was trying to outrun myself, to reach a place where my death couldn't touch me. Because isn't that what it's about, this restlessness? If I keep moving, I can trick myself into believing I'm alive.

*

The average lifespan for an American man born the year my son was, 2008, is 75.5 years. For an American man born in 1921, as was my opponent's father, the average was 60; for a woman born in 1924, as was his wife, it was 61.5. In January of 2013, my opponent's father celebrated his 92nd birthday; in 2003, his wife died of a sudden stroke at the age of 78. Had either been born in Japan, Switzerland, or even Italy, their lives might have been slightly longer. Had either been born in Sierra Leone, Lesotho, or the Democratic Republic of Congo, their lives would have been, with little doubt, much shorter. Born in Minnesota in 1953, my opponent's life expectancy is 72. Born in Connecticut in 1979, my own, perversely, is 70.

*

Never ones to waste a perfectly good tradition, the early Christians scheduled Easter near the vernal equinox. The overlap with Passover was no coincidence. I remember as a child hearing from the priest in the pulpit that belief came down to this. He may have said something about sin, but all I remember is the resurrection. The dead had not only been brought back to life but in a familiar form and in far less time than it takes to read the accounts. I wake early, as usual, and check in on the game, nearing its end on a day of new beginnings. Over the phone, my opponent tells me she is praying for mercy. But we never talk about the game. We aren't talking about it now. There is, she says, no end in sight.

*

For months we planned our move. My wife transferred her licensure, applied for jobs. We spoke to realtors, browsed the listings, and made our peace with difficult summers. Retirees. Amusement parks. We convinced ourselves there were things to like about Florida, even things we might like about it. March turned into April, April into May, and suddenly I was about to leave on a house-hunting trip. There were plans in the works for a dinner with my future colleagues. I was to take part in a curriculum retreat. And then something happened. I didn't make that dinner. I didn't board that plane. A few days before I was to leave, as I was grading my last batch of student writing for the year, I got another phone call. It was the chair of my current department. Something had come up, he said, and he wanted to know: was there any way I would consider staying?

*

In a zero-sum game you gain nothing from winning, except the pleasure of it. Victory is achieved at your opponent's expense: you win because they lose. But a lot depends on that *nothing*. I compete with my opponent, and though I want to win I can only do so, as this is not a game for one, with her cooperation. She calls the game a way to keep in touch, an invisible umbilicus reaching through time and space to connect, for example, a mother with her grown son. Much has been made of our connectivity, of the profound linkages that join us, through technology, to the world, but it's sometimes nothing more than a game, albeit one in which winning and losing, or living and dying, are not the right words.

*

Pema Chödrön tells the story of a woman being chased by tigers. Clinging to a vine, she climbs down a cliff to escape. But as she descends, she sees there are also tigers below. Worse yet, a mouse is chewing through the vine. She then notices a tiny patch of strawberries growing on the mountainside. Tigers above, tigers below, she's nonetheless delighted. She reaches out. The fruit is pulpy and sweet.

*

At the end of this story I'm not back at the beginning exactly. It's more like I'm back in the middle, teaching the same book in the same classroom where, in late April of 2012, I taught a sample class for the job that would later turn into the one I have now. I begin today's session on the exercise with which I ended that earlier one. I ask the group to raise their hands— a quick straw poll, I say—if they've ever done anything stupid. There's the usual laughter, and when they all have their hands in the air I ask them to brainstorm a list of five foolish things they've done. Then I ask them to choose one and to tell it as a story that begins, like the memoir from which the exercise is drawn, Deb Olin Unferth's *Revolution*, at the end.

Today, as I'm sketching my own account, I understand for the first time that the exercise proceeds from a faulty premise. It assumes an ending for any particular situation, as though one's actions, the choices made and unmade, didn't reverberate through time. The story continues, even if—or because—it has to end.

*

The inevitable *no*'s and *it*'s and *uh*'s litter the board. The plays are feeble because the material is. Not only have the best letters been taken, the real estate is limited. Even if I could spell *emotion*, there wouldn't be any place for it. Most games sputter out like this. There's no dramatic flourish, no deathbed revelations. I play my *n* on a double-word score, spelling both *in* and *en*.

*

Sometimes words aren't much more than placeholders, like saying *thingamajig* when you mean the mechanism that connects the gas line to the stove. Other times, they betray our true intentions. I say *the market's been good to me* or *I'm on the market again this year*, and in each instance I subordinate myself to commerce. The self in each sentence is one in a larger supply of selves, but is there demand? Or am I surplus? I can't stay with these thoughts for long before I recognize how many parts of my life have been shaped into various economies. I have an economy of time, of pleasure, of consumption and elimination, even an economy of affection. How much time do I have to spend today, how much time do I have to save? How much attention can I give to my family, and how much of theirs do I require? You can't set a price on these things, but that's just my point: I do it anyway. Capital is a powerful lens. Still, there's something to be said about the fact that all my efforts at acquiring the job I wanted led me to one I couldn't have planned for, that the market in which I sought security was not necessarily the same as the community that has, for now, provided it. There's also something to be said about all the sleep my wife and I lost anticipating realities that didn't come to pass. The truths these sentences point to are familiar ones—I won't belabor them. Except to say that when I finished my career report all those years ago, I couldn't have predicted that more than two decades later I would recognize so much of myself in it: "Mr. Gunther had a hard job, but he loved it."

*

In nature, nothing is wasted. Not only has every one of my atoms been a part of several stars, each one has been a part of a million other living things. I may be materially a mongrel, but I am also, on the atomic level, part and parcel of the fabric of the cosmos. It's almost certain that some of my atoms once belonged to the Buddha, to Walt Whitman, to Genghis Khan. Eventually my matter—fused together for now—will split apart, only to fuse again into billions of new arrangements.

*

When the game is over, there is never any question of a rematch. We begin again. And again. And again.

ACKNOWLEDGMENTS

Many of these essays first appeared elsewhere, and in each instance the generosity and perspicacity of the editors invariably improved the work along the way:

3:AM Magazine: "Certified Copies"
Los Angeles Review of Books: "The Sum of Two Cubes (And the Uses of Literature)"
Seneca Review: "In the Anthropocene" (as "In the Holocene")
Something on Paper: "For a Body Not to Be"
Tammy: "Anything Other Than Everything"
Unstuck: "The Language of Nim"
Terrain.org: "The Rise of Slime"
West Branch: "A Kind of Cuba"
Your Impossible Voice: "Letter from Lancaster"
Zone 3: "Flutter Point"

"The Sum of Two Cubes (And the Uses of Literature)" was originally presented as a lecture during the 2012 Naropa University Summer Writing Program.

Writing, like thinking, is a social, collaborative act, and I am fortunate for the many people who contributed to the shapes of these essays, and to the thinking they entailed. Thanks to Barb Anderson, Scott Anderson, J'Lyn Chapman, Allen Collins, Dave Enno, Chatarina Eskered, Scott Howard, Peter Jaros, Mike Kroll, Sue Kroll, Elizabeth Lonsdorf, Antonio Marques, Padmini Mongia, Nick Montemarano, Virginia Morell, Jeremy

Moss, Leigh Moss, Judith Mueller, Broc Russell, Jeff Steinbrink, and Brenna Stuart. Special thanks to David Bieloh and Susan Wallace for all of their work in bringing this book together. To Hilary Plum, for her keen eyes and good ear (yet again). To Amy Wright, for believing in and supporting my work through the years. And to Amy Fusselman, for saying yes: it's a rare enough experience to win anything, in the writing world or beyond it—what an honor to have this book selected by a writer whose work I have long admired. Finally, for their love and support and patience, endless thanks to Susan and Elias.